CASSEROLE COOKING

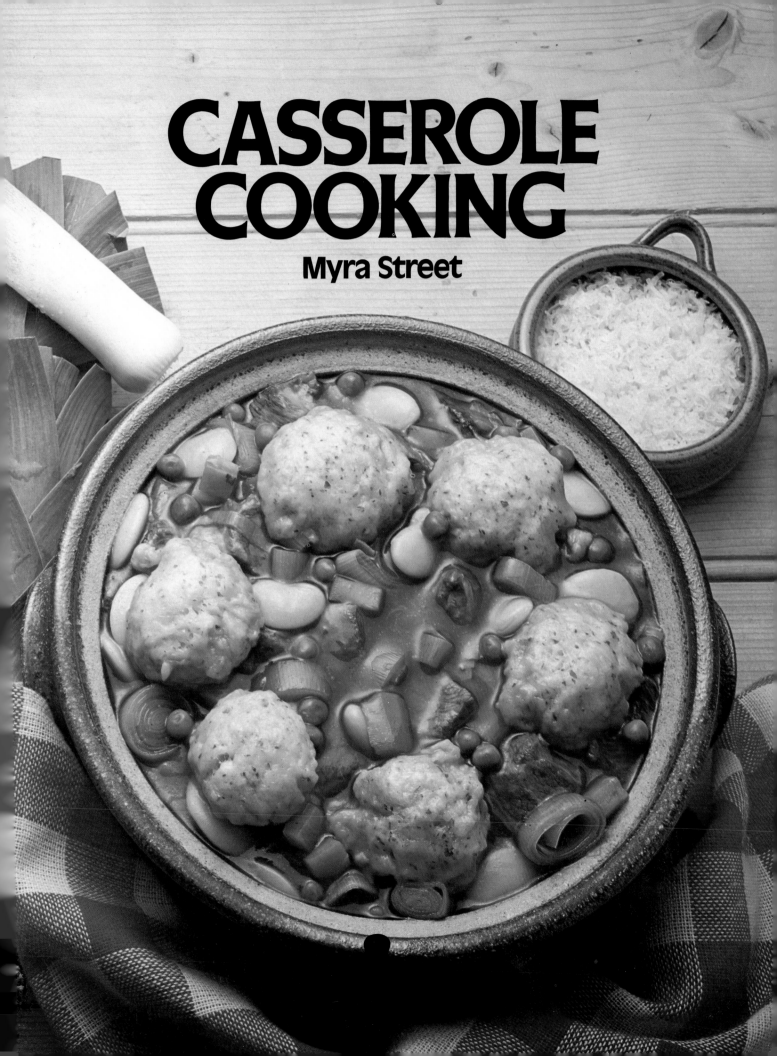

CASSEROLE COOKING
Myra Street

Contents

This edition first published in 1978 by
Octopus Books Limited
59 Grosvenor Street, London W1

© 1977 Hennerwood Publications Limited

ISBN 0 7064 0770 9

Produced by Mandarin Publishers Limited,
22a Westlands Road, Quarry Bay, Hong Kong

Printed in Hong Kong

Introduction

It is perhaps extraordinary to think that the words "casserole" and "stew" mean exactly the same, for they conjure up two entirely different concepts in most people's minds. One thinks of a casserole as being French and exotic, rich in flavor and served in an attractive dish. A stew on the other hand, brings to mind cheap cuts of meat which, cooked in any other way, might well be tough. Some of us possibly remember the stew of school meals as being uninteresting and tasteless, but there is no reason why it shouldn't be as flavorsome as any exciting French casserole.

The essence of casserole cooking is the relatively slow cooking of a mixture of ingredients and a small amount of liquid, in a dish which has a close fitting lid. The fit of the lid is important as it ensures the richness of the result and the minimal loss of liquid. Ideally, too, the casserole dish should distribute heat well and evenly, so that food doesn't stick on the bottom. This is why the enameled cast iron casseroles are so popular. China, pottery, earthenware and heat resistant glass are all satisfactory, although much more fragile; and it is not a good thing to have any cracks in dishes as they not only harbor germs but often allow liquids to exude.

Nowadays the range and choice of casseroles are marvelous and can add enormously to the look of the table and the pleasure of eating. Before using a particular type of dish, check first that it is suitable for the method of cooking chosen. Some are not suitable for cooking on top of the range so care must be taken.

Mention should also be made of the slow cooking crockpots that are now marketed by several manufacturers. Do be careful to follow the manufacturer's instructions and in particular note that some of these cookers must be pre-heated before any ingredients are put in, and the stock or liquid to be used should be brought to boil before adding.

The two main advantages of these new cookers are that they are said to be economical, using little electricity, and they cook very slowly, which is useful if you are likely to be out all day. They are also good for the tougher cuts of meat which need very slow cooking.

Whatever type of container you use, remember that casseroles are ideal for using in conjunction with automatic ovens, but it is advisable to add another quarter or half an hour to the cooking time in order to allow the oven to warm up.

Cold start casserole

In nearly all the recipes given in this book, I have recommended that the meat to be casseroled should first be browned in butter, fat or oil, as this gives a better looking and better tasting result. It is possible – and advisable if the meat is one of the tougher cuts – to cook the meat very slowly without browning first.

Freezing

Frozen meat must be thawed if the recipe states that the meat must first be browned. All poultry and game must be thawed before using in any type of cooked dish as harmful bacteria can lurk near the bone. If the flesh around the bone is still frozen when the bird is cooked, the heat may not penetrate fully and harmful bacteria will not be killed off by the high temperature but may even multiply in the warmth.

Cooked casseroles can be reheated directly from the frozen state and a quantity for 4 persons will take $1-1\frac{1}{2}$ hours to reheat thoroughly at $325°F$.

Packing casseroles for the freezer

Pyrex containers can be used in the freezer and are suitable for using direct from freezer to oven. This also applies to foil containers and metal containers. However few of us have enough freezer space or enough casseroles to leave the meat in the containers. The best way is to freeze in the casserole, then turn out onto double thickness foil and seal well. Label each casserole with the contents and the description of the casserole and it can then be put back into the same casserole for reheating without any difficulty from awkward frozen shapes.

Casseroles flavored with herbs, wine and spices, do tend to change flavor in the freezer. Over 3–4 weeks this is not too noticeable but over several months you may find that you have to adjust the flavorings when reheating. Under-cook casseroles to be frozen by half an hour.

Cooking meat in bulk for casseroles pays dividends in time and kitchen mess. Several pounds of beef, lamb, pork or veal can be browned at one session, casseroled with chopped onions and seasoning for 1 hour then divided in 2, 4, 6 or 8 portions. Prepare vegetables and herbs and cook as for a freshly made casserole.

Cooking times for casseroles depend very much on the quality of meat used and to some extent the casserole dish itself, so always test

your casseroles at the minimum time given to make sure the meat does not become overcooked.

Thickening and stock for casseroles

Casseroles are interesting and creative to make, as the flavor can always be varied to suit the mood of the cook. Basically meat or poultry, vegetables, herbs, seasoning and stock are the ingredients. A change of herb or vegetable can transform the basic brown stew or chicken casserole into an exciting meal to suit the individual tastes of each family. Thickening for a casserole is dependent on individual taste. Some people prefer thicker consistencies to others and the easiest way to deal with this is with "beurre manié". This is butter and flour kneaded together and used for thickening gravies. This method helps to give a glossy sauce and is I think more palatable than cornstarch.

The stock used in the recipes can either be made as directed at the beginning of the beef, poultry or fish sections if time and ingredients are available. Alternatively bouillon cubes can be made up with water and used as directed. Remember though that these can be salty.

The following terms appear in the recipes and it is a good idea to understand their meaning.
Baste To spoon fat or liquid over food.
Beurre manié Kneaded butter and flour mixture for thickening sauces, ragoûts, stews and casseroles. Use 2 parts butter to 1 part flour and work into a paste. Add to the liquid in small pieces and whisk or stir well. Some people find it easier to add liquid to beurre manié, blend, and return to the main part of the sauce. Use 2 tablespoons butter, 2 tablespoons flour, 2½ cups liquid.
Blanch To whiten or to plunge into cold water and bring to the boil. With green vegetables plunge into boiling water for 1 minute before cooking by another method.
Bouquet garni A collection of herbs in a small muslin or cheesecloth bag. 1 bay leaf, sprig of thyme, 3 parsley stalks. May be tied together and removed after cooking if muslin is not available.
Fry To cook over a brisk heat to obtain a good seal and a good color.
Marinate To soak meat, poultry or game in oil, vinegar or wine and vegetables before cooking.
Roux Another important thickening agent made by melting butter in a saucepan and adding the flour to make a ball of dough which is known as the "roux". White roux is used for white sauces accompanying veal, chicken and fish dishes. Blond roux, where butter is browned slightly, is used for chicken and fish.

Brown roux is made by cooking flour in the butter until a rich brown color is obtained. The hot liquid is then added gradually. Excellent for brown stews and dark sauces in casseroles.
Sauté To fry gently for a golden result.
Sweat To cook vegetables or meat in a little fat over very low heat to avoid browning.
All spoon measurements are level.
All recipes serve four unless otherwise stated.

There are several points to look for when choosing beef, whether it is for the casserole, the roasting pan, frying pan or grill. Good beef is a deep red color with a marbling of fat through it. It is this marbling which helps to give the beef its flavor and tenderness. Dark browny red, dried beef has been exposed to the air too long.
Suitable cuts of beef for the casserole: Chuck, Rump, Sirloin tip, Shoulder, Boneless neck, Top and bottom round.
To make Beef stock place 2–3 lbs of chopped beef bones, preferably with some marrow bone, in a saucepan with 1–2 quarts water, 1 onion, 1 carrot, 1 small piece of turnip or celery, bouquet garni and some peppercorns. Bring to the boil and simmer until liquid is reduced by half. Strain and then remove fat when cool.
Alternatively make in a pressure cooker.
To freeze stock: Place in 1 or 2 containers, remove and pack in plastic bags for easy storage. Small cubes may be made in ice-cube trays and transferred to plastic bags when frozen.

Hamburgers with orange sauce

4 hamburgers
2 medium-sized onions, peeled and sliced
1 tablespoon vegetable oil
1 tablespoon butter
1 teaspoon flour
⅔ cup orange juice, fresh or canned
1 teaspoon finely grated orange
rind (optional)
½ teaspoon Worcestershire sauce
1 tablespoon wine vinegar
1 tablespoon tomato paste
4 canned tomatoes, drained
Salt and freshly ground black pepper

To garnish:
Blanched orange rind
Watercress sprigs

Cooking Time: 30 minutes
Oven: 325°F

Brown the hamburgers and sauté the onions gently in the oil. Place in a casserole. Make a roux with the butter and flour, add the orange juice, Worcestershire sauce, vinegar and tomato paste. Cook well, stir in the tomatoes and season well. Pour into the casserole and cook for 20 minutes. Taste and adjust the seasoning before serving. Decorate with blanched orange rind, cut into strips and watercress sprigs. Serve with baked potatoes and a crisp green salad with slices or segments of orange.

Beef in beer

2 onions, peeled and diced
2 carrots, peeled and sliced
4 mushrooms, washed and sliced
3 tablespoons oil
1 lb stewing beef, cubed
1 tablespoon seasoned flour
2 tablespoons tomato paste
⅔ cup beer
Salt and freshly ground black pepper
1 teaspoon thyme
1 bay leaf

To garnish:
Triangles of toast
6 parsley sprigs (optional)

Cooking Time: 1½–2 hours
Oven: 350°F

Sweat the vegetables in 2 tablespoons oil for 5 minutes. Remove from heat and place into a casserole. Toss the meat in the flour and fry until brown over a brisk heat, adding the remaining oil. Place on top of the vegetables, pour over the tomato paste mixed with the beer, seasoning and herbs. Cook, covered, in the oven for 1½ hours. Remove the bay leaf, taste and adjust the seasoning. Garnish with triangles of toast and sprigs of parsley, if liked.

Hamburgers with orange sauce; Beef in beer

Beef and lentil stew

2 tablespoons oil
1 lb stewing beef, trimmed of fat and
cut into 1 inch cubes
1 onion, peeled and diced
1 carrot, scraped and diced
⅔ cup lentils, soaked in 2 cups beef stock
Salt and freshly ground black pepper
½ teaspoon mustard
½ teaspoon Worcestershire sauce
16 oz can tomatoes
½ teaspoon basil
1 bay leaf
½ teaspoon sugar

Cooking time: 1½ hours
Oven: 325°F

Heat the oil in a frying pan and fry meat until browned and sealed. Transfer to casserole. Sauté vegetables until transparent and slightly browned, add to casserole. Add lentils soaked in stock, seasoning, chopped tomatoes and juice, herbs and sugar. Bring to just below boiling and pour over the meat in the casserole. Cook for 1–1½ hours. Remove bay leaf. Taste and adjust seasoning. Serve with a crisp green vegetable.

Braised sliced beef

2 medium-sized carrots, peeled and diced
1 small turnip, peeled and diced
1 large onion, peeled and diced
1 medium-sized parsnip, peeled and diced
1 medium-sized leek, well washed
and sliced
1 clove garlic, crushed
3 tablespoons oil
1½ lbs stewing beef, cut into
3 inch × 2 inch slices
Bouquet garni
Salt and freshly ground black pepper
2½ cups stock
⅔ cup red wine
2 teaspoons Worcestershire sauce
Parsley sprigs to garnish

Cooking Time: 2½ hours
Oven: 300°F

Sauté the vegetables in 1 tablespoon of the oil, and place in the bottom of a casserole. Brown the meat in the remaining oil and arrange over the vegetables. Add the bouquet garni and season well. Mix the stock, wine and Worcestershire sauce and pour over. Cover and cook in oven for 2–2¼ hours. Taste and adjust the seasoning and remove bouquet garni before serving, garnish with parsley sprigs.

Beef and lentil stew; Braised sliced beef; Beef cobbler

Beef cobbler

4 tablespoons oil
1 lb stewing beef, trimmed and cut into
small cubes
1 tablespoon seasoned flour
2 onions, peeled and diced
2 carrots, peeled and diced
1 small turnip, peeled and diced
1 bay leaf
Salt and freshly ground black pepper
2 cups beef stock

Scone topping:
1 cup flour
$\frac{1}{4}$ teaspoon salt
4 tablespoons margarine
$\frac{1}{4}$ teaspoon dried thyme
1 egg
2 tablespoons milk

Cooking Time: 1$\frac{1}{2}$ hours
Oven: 350°F then increase to 425°F

Heat half the oil in a frying pan or casserole. Toss the meat in the flour and fry until golden brown on a fairly high heat. Turn down the heat, add remaining oil and vegetables, and sauté gently for a few minutes. Add the bay leaf, seasoning and stock and bring to the boil. Place in a casserole, if you have used a frying pan, cover and cook for 1 hour in the oven. Meanwhile sift the flour and salt, then rub in the fat until the mixture resembles fine breadcrumbs. Add the herbs and mix with the egg and milk to a soft dough. Roll out on a floured board until the dough is 1 inch thick and cut into rounds or triangles. Remove casserole from the oven, taste and adjust the seasoning. Turn up the heat and arrange scones on top, return to the top shelf of the oven for 15 minutes or until scone topping is golden brown.

BEEF
Carbonnade of beef

1½ lbs lean beef, rump or chuck, trimmed or cut into 2 inch slices
1 tablespoon flour
Salt and freshly ground black pepper
2 oz slab bacon, rinded and diced
4 tablespoons butter
1 tablespoon oil
3 large onions, peeled and thinly sliced
1¼ cups brown ale
1¼ cups beef stock
1 teaspoon Dijon mustard
Bouquet garni
8 slices French bread
4 teaspoons Dijon mustard

To finish:
Parsley sprigs

Cooking Time: 1¾–2 hours
Oven: 350°F

Toss steak in seasoned flour. Brown bacon in butter and oil and transfer to a casserole. Sauté onions in a frying pan then brown the beef on both sides, place in the casserole with the onions. Sprinkle remaining flour in the pan. Add ale, stock, and scrape juices from pan. Add to casserole with mustard and bouquet garni. Cook for 1½ hours in the oven or until tender. Remove bouquet garni. Taste and adjust seasoning, and consistency, if desired. Place French bread, spread with mustard on the top. Cook, uncovered, for a further 15–20 minutes. Garnish with parsley sprigs.

Carbonnade of beef

Red pepper and beef casserole

1 lb stewing beef, trimmed and cut into
1½ inch cubes
2 tablespoons oil
2 tablespoons butter
1 large onion, peeled and sliced
1 small carrot, peeled and sliced
1 thick slice bacon, diced
1 stalk celery, washed and sliced
1 red pepper, washed and diced
6 mushrooms, washed and sliced
1 cup canned peeled tomatoes
4 bay leaves
¼ teaspoon dried marjoram
Salt and freshly ground black pepper
1 cup boiling water
1 beef bouillon cube
4 tablespoons red wine

Cooking Time: 1½–1¾ hours
Oven: 325°F

Fry the meat in hot oil, cooking quickly to ensure a good rich colour. Remove to a casserole. Add the butter to the pan and heat up. Sauté the onion, carrot, bacon and celery. Place over the meat, together with the pepper, mushrooms, tomatoes, herbs and seasoning. Make up the stock from the water and bouillon cube, add the red wine and pour over the casserole. Cover with a lid and cook for 1–1½ hours. Remove bay leaves. Taste and adjust seasoning before serving. Thicken with beurre manié if liked (see page 7).

Red pepper and beef casserole

Tomato beef curry

1 lb stewing beef, trimmed and cut into
1 inch cubes
2 tablespoons oil
1 tablespoon butter
1 large onion, peeled and sliced
1 carrot, peeled and sliced
2 tablespoons curry powder
1 tablespoon flour
1 tablespoon turmeric
16 oz can tomatoes
1¼–2 cups stock
Salt
4 bay leaves

Cooking Time: 1¾ hours
Oven: 325°F

Brown the meat in the oil over a high flame. Add the butter and sauté the onion and carrot until tender. Remove to a casserole with the meat. Add curry powder, flour, and turmeric and fry for 2 minutes. Stir in the tomatoes and stock. Cook and keep stirring from time to time until all juices are removed from the bottom of the pan. Season well with salt. Add to the casserole with the bay leaves. Cover and put in the oven to cook for 1½ hours. Remove bay leaves and taste and adjust seasoning before serving.

Madras meat and vegetable curry

1 onion, peeled and diced
2 tablespoons oil
1 lb chuck, trimmed and cubed
1 tablespoon flour
1 clove garlic, crushed
1–2 tablespoons Madras curry powder
¼ teaspoon chilli powder (optional)
1¼ cups beef stock
1 teaspoon tomato paste
1 potato, peeled and diced
½ teaspoon salt
4 cauliflower flowerets

To garnish:
1 small onion, peeled and sliced

Cooking Time: 1¾ hours
Oven: 325°F

Sauté the onion in oil, gently, and remove to a casserole. Toss the cubes of beef in flour and fry over a fairly high heat to brown. When brown lower the heat, add the crushed garlic and sprinkle with curry powder and chilli and allow to sauté for a few minutes. Pour on the stock mixed with tomato paste and transfer to the casserole when liquid begins to simmer. Add the potato, cover and simmer for 1 hour, add the salt. Add cauliflower and cover for the last 25–30 minutes of cooking. Taste and adjust seasoning before serving. Garnish with thinly sliced onion rings.
Accompaniments for curry are easy to obtain from the many Asian stores throughout the country.

Serve curries with:
Boiled or fried rice
Fried poppadums
Chapati – flat pancakes made from
brown flour
Cucumber Raita – plain yogurt
with chopped cucumber
Sliced bananas, soaked in lemon juice
Mango chutney
Thinly sliced onion and tomato salad or
thinly sliced onion, tomato, and
green pepper salad
Toasted coconut

Tomato beef curry; Madras meat and vegetable curry

Celery beef casserole with walnuts

1 lb stewing beef, trimmed and cut into
1 inch cubes
2 tablespoons oil
2 onions, peeled and diced
1 carrot, peeled and diced
1 tablespoon butter
1 tablespoon flour
1¼ cups beef stock
Salt and freshly ground black pepper
1 head celery, washed and sliced into
1 inch lengths
½ teaspoon dried basil
1 tablespoon sour cream
¼ cup walnuts, chopped

Cooking Time: 1½–2 hours
Oven: 300°F

Brown the meat in the oil and place in a casserole. Sauté the onions and carrots in the butter in the frying pan. Add the flour to make a roux and gradually add the stock, stirring with a wooden spoon until a smooth sauce is formed. Season well and pour over the meat. Add the celery and basil. Cover and cook in the oven for 1½–1¾ hours. Just before serving taste and adjust the seasoning, add the sour cream and sprinkle with chopped walnuts.

Alabama chilli

Alabama chilli

1 tablespoon oil
1 lb ground beef
2 onions, peeled and diced
1 carrot, peeled and diced
1 pepper, seeded and diced
1 chilli, seeded and diced
16 oz can tomatoes
2–3 tablespoons tomato paste
⅔ cup stock
1 bay leaf
½ teaspoon chilli powder
½ teaspoon dried thyme
Salt and freshly ground black pepper
1 package frozen whole kernel corn
15¼ oz can kidney beans, drained

Cooking Time: 1 hour

Heat the oil in a frying pan and brown the meat. Transfer to a casserole. Sauté the onions, carrot, pepper and chilli and add to the meat. Add the remaining ingredients except for the sweet corn and kidney beans, season well. Bring to the boil and simmer over a low heat for 45 minutes. Add the sweet corn and kidney beans and simmer for a further 15 minutes. Remove the bay leaf, taste and adjust the seasoning. Chilli powder may be adjusted to taste; a mild mixture will only require ¼ teaspoon. Serve with boiled rice or pasta.

Celery beef casserole with walnuts; Farmer's casserole

Farmer's casserole

2 tablespoons oil
1 lb stewing beef, trimmed and cut into
1 inch cubes
2 carrots, peeled and diced
2 leeks, washed and sliced
1 onion, peeled and diced
1 tablespoon butter
1¼ cups beef stock
Salt and freshly ground black pepper
1¾ cups canned lima beans, drained
½ cup frozen peas

For the cheese dumplings:
1 cup self rising flour
2 oz suet, shredded
1 teaspoon finely chopped parsley
½ cup finely grated cheese
Water to mix

Cooking Time: 1½–2 hours
Oven: 350°F

Heat the oil in a frying pan and brown the meat. Transfer to a casserole. Sauté the vegetables in the butter in the frying pan and add to the meat. Stir in the stock and season well. Cover and cook in the oven for 1 hour. Meanwhile make the dumplings by putting all the dry ingredients in a bowl and mixing together with a little water to form a soft dough. Shape into 12 small dumplings. Remove the casserole from the oven. Stir in the lima beans and peas. Taste and adjust the seasoning. Arrange the dumplings over the top and put the uncovered casserole back in the oven for 30 minutes or until the dumplings are golden brown.

Mexican beef

4 scallions, washed and chopped
4 tablespoons white wine
2 tablespoons wine vinegar
Salt and freshly ground black pepper
1 teaspoon fresh tarragon
4 hamburgers
1 avocado pear, halved, half diced and
half thinly sliced
1 tablespoon oil
½ teaspoon chilli powder, or to taste
2 tablespoons butter
1 onion, peeled and sliced
1 teaspoon flour
2 tablespoons lemon juice

To garnish:
Tarragon sprigs (optional)

Cooking Time: 30 minutes

Make a marinade with the scallions, wine, vinegar, seasoning and tarragon. Marinate the hamburgers for several hours. Remove and add the diced avocado to marinade. Heat the oil in a casserole, sprinkle with chilli powder and brown hamburgers quickly on each side. Add the butter and onion and sweat for a few minutes, sprinkle with flour and brown, pour in the strained marinade and cook for 15 minutes. Add the diced avocado and stir in gently. Taste and adjust the seasoning. Arrange the remaining slices of avocado on top of the meat, sprinkle with lemon juice and cook for a further 10 minutes. Garnish with fresh tarragon, if available.

Rough puff pastry

1¾ cups flour
½ teaspoon salt
12 tablespoons margarine or butter
1 teaspoon lemon juice
6–8 tablespoons water

Cooking Time: 10–15 minutes
Oven: 425°F

Sift the flour and salt together into a mixing bowl. Cut the fat into small pieces, add to the flour and toss lightly so that each piece of fat is coated with flour. Add the lemon juice and water to the flour and fat and mix lightly with the blade of a knife making sure the pieces of fat are kept whole. If any loose flour remains, add a little more water and mix until the dough is soft. Gather the dough with the fingertips. Turn out onto a well floured board and sprinkle with flour.
Form into an oblong, flour the rolling pin and roll out to a strip about 15 inches by 13 inches. Fold in 3 by folding the bottom third of the pastry upwards and the top third downwards and over the bottom fold.
Lightly press the three edges together with a rolling pin to seal.
Turn the pastry round so that the sealed right-hand edge faces you. Roll out to an oblong as before.
Brush off any surplus flour. Fold in three again and seal the edges. Sprinkle with flour, cover with a damp cloth and leave in a cool place for 20 minutes, until cool and firm.

Third and fourth rollings
Repeat as in second rolling a third and fourth time. After the last rolling and resting, the pastry is ready to roll out again to the required thickness and use.

Oranged steak and kidney casserole

2 tablespoons oil
1 onion, peeled and sliced
4 mushrooms, washed and sliced
1 lb stewing beef, trimmed and cut into
1 inch cubes
½ lb kidney, cleaned, cored and sliced
Finely grated rind of 1 orange
⅔ cup stock
Salt and freshly ground black pepper
1 tablespoon cornstarch

To garnish:
1 tablespoon finely chopped parsley
Squares of puff pastry or rough
puff pastry

Cooking Time: 1¾ hours
Oven: 325°F

Heat the oil in a frying pan, sauté the onion and mushrooms in the oil for 3–4 minutes. Drain well and place in a casserole. Brown the beef and kidney over a fairly high heat to obtain good colour. Then place on top of vegetables. Add the grated orange rind, stock and seasoning to the frying pan and bring to the boil. Pour over the meat and vegetables. Cover the casserole and cook for 1½ hours. Blend the cornstarch with a little water and thicken gravy, taste and adjust seasoning. Sprinkle with the parsley. Serve with squares of cooked puff or rough puff pastry.

Mexican beef; Oranged steak and kidney casserole

Goulash

2 tablespoons oil
1 lb stewing beef, trimmed and cubed
2 teaspoons paprika
2 teaspoons flour
1¼ cups beef stock
2 tablespoons butter
½ lb onions, peeled and diced
½ lb carrots, scrubbed and diced
1 bay leaf
Good pinch of thyme
16 oz can tomatoes
1 tablespoon tomato paste
1 teaspoon lemon juice
Salt and freshly ground black pepper
1 potato, peeled and diced
8 small onions, peeled
1 tablespoon sour cream

To garnish:
1 tablespoon finely chopped parsley

Cooking Time: 1¾–2 hours
Oven: 325°F

Heat the oil in a frying pan over a fairly high heat and fry the meat until brown on all sides. Reduce the heat, sprinkle with paprika and flour, turn the meat over to absorb the flour. After about 2–3 minutes pour the stock into the frying pan and stir gently. Pour into a casserole with the meat and meat particles. Rinse the pan, melt the butter and sweat the onions and carrots gently over a low heat. Add herbs, tomatoes, tomato paste, lemon juice and seasoning. The potato can be made into balls or diced at this stage and added to the tomato mixture. Pour tomato mixture over the meat in the casserole and cook in the oven for 1 hour. Remove casserole, add small onions and return for an additional 45 minutes. Before serving remove bay leaf, taste and adjust the seasoning, stir in sour cream and sprinkle with parsley.

Herbed beef casserole

2 tablespoons oil
1 large onion, peeled and sliced
1 large carrot, peeled and sliced
1 lb stewing steak, trimmed and cut into
1½ inch cubes
2 mushrooms, washed and sliced
1 stalk celery, washed and sliced
1 cup canned peeled tomatoes
1 tablespoon tomato paste
1 teaspoon tarragon
1 teaspoon oregano
1 bay leaf
Salt and freshly ground black pepper
1 cup boiling water
1 beef bouillon cube

Beurre manié
2 tablespoons butter blended with
2 tablespoons flour

Cooking Time: 1¾ hours
Oven: 325°F

Preheat the oven. Heat the oil in a frying pan and fry the onion and carrot until the onion is soft. Remove the vegetables and place in a casserole. Brown the meat quickly in the hot fat to seal in the juices, then add to the vegetables, together with mushrooms and celery. Add tomatoes, tomato paste and herbs. Season with salt and pepper. Make up the stock from the water and bouillon cube and pour over the contents of the casserole. Cover with the lid and place in the oven for 1½ hours. Taste and adjust seasoning and thicken with a beurre manié before serving.

Herbed beef casserole; Goulash

Fluffy meatloaf casserole

1 tablespoon oil
2 tablespoons butter
2 onions, peeled and diced
4 oz mushrooms, washed and
chopped (optional)
1 lb lean ground beef
1 tablespoon flour
$\frac{2}{3}$ cup stock
2 teaspoons Worcestershire sauce
$\frac{1}{2}$ teaspoon dried thyme
Salt and freshly ground black pepper
$\frac{3}{4}$ lb cooked, mashed potatoes
2 eggs, separated
$\frac{1}{4}$ cup grated cheese

Cooking Time: 1 hour
Oven: 375°F

Heat the oil and butter in a frying pan and sauté the onions and mushrooms for about 4 minutes. Remove to a casserole, brown the ground beef, sprinkle with flour, add the stock, Worcestershire sauce and seasoning and simmer for a few minutes, then pour into the casserole. Beat the potatoes with seasoning and egg yolks until creamy and free from lumps. Whisk the egg whites until light and fluffy and fold into the potatoes. Fork on to the meat mixture, sprinkle with grated cheese and cook on the middle shelf of the oven for 45 minutes.

Fluffy meatloaf casserole; Highland casserole

Highland casserole

2 tablespoons oil
1 lb stewing beef, trimmed and cut into
1 inch cubes
2 onions, peeled and diced
1 carrot, peeled and diced
1 turnip, peeled and diced
$\frac{1}{4}$ cup pearl barley
1 tablespoon Worcestershire sauce
2 cups beef stock
2 bay leaves
Salt and freshly ground black pepper

To garnish:
Chopped parsley

Cooking Time: $1\frac{1}{2}$–$1\frac{3}{4}$ hours
Oven: 350°F

Heat the oil in a frying pan and brown the meat. Lower heat, add the vegetables and cook for about 3 minutes. Transfer to a casserole and add the remaining ingredients. Cover and cook for $1\frac{1}{2}$ hours. Taste and adjust the seasoning, remove bay leaves, and serve garnished with chopped parsley.

Beef provençale

Beef provençale

2 tablespoons oil
1 lb stewing beef, trimmed and cut into
1 inch cubes
1½ onions, peeled and sliced
¼ red or green pepper, seeded and diced
1 large tomato, washed and sliced
1 large carrot, scraped and diced
4 small mushrooms
1 thick slice bacon, diced
2 tablespoons butter

Stock:
⅔ cup water
4 tablespoons red wine
1 teaspoon tomato paste
2 teaspoons salt
1 teaspoon oregano
1 teaspoon thyme
Freshly ground black pepper

Cooking Time: 1¾–2 hours
Oven: 325°F

Heat the oil in a frying pan and fry meat until browned and sealed. Transfer to a casserole dish. Fry all the vegetables and the bacon gently in the butter in the frying pan. When the vegetables are soft, add contents of frying pan to the casserole. Make up the stock by placing all the ingredients given in a saucepan and bringing to the boil. Add to the casserole. Place in the oven for 1½–1¾ hours. Taste and adjust the seasoning, thicken with beurre manié if necessary before serving (see page 7).

Italian beef casserole

1 medium-sized onion, peeled and sliced
1 large carrot, scraped and diced
2 tablespoons oil
1 lb stewing beef, trimmed and cut into
1 inch cubes
2 mushrooms, washed and sliced
1 cup canned tomatoes
$\frac{1}{4}$ red pepper, seeded and sliced
1 cup boiling water
1 beef bouillon cube
1 tablespoon tomato paste
$\frac{1}{2}$ teaspoon oregano
1 bay leaf
Salt and freshly ground black pepper
1 tablespoon flour
1 tablespoon butter

Cooking Time: 1$\frac{1}{2}$ hours
Oven: 325°F

Sauté vegetables in the oil until tender. Drain and place in the bottom of a casserole. Fry the meat until brown to seal in the juices. Place on top of the vegetables. Lay the mushrooms on top of the meat. Add the tomatoes to the casserole. Place the sliced pepper over the mushrooms. Make up the stock with the water and bouillon cube, add tomato paste and pour in. Add the oregano and bay leaf, season well and stir to mix. Cover and put into the oven. Remove after 1 hour and taste and adjust the seasoning. Thicken with a beurre manié (see page 7), make sure gravy is smooth and free from lumps and continue cooking for a further 15–20 minutes or until meat is tender. Remove the bay leaf before serving.

Burgundian beef

1 lb rump beef, trimmed and cut into
1 inch cubes
2 onions, peeled and thinly sliced
2 carrots, peeled and thinly sliced
6 peppercorns
3 parsley sprigs
$\frac{1}{4}$ teaspoon dried thyme
1 bay leaf
1$\frac{1}{4}$ cups red wine
2 tablespoons oil
2 tablespoons butter
16 small white onions
2 thick slices bacon, cut into strips
2 tablespoons brandy
2 tablespoons flour
1 clove garlic, crushed
$\frac{2}{3}$ cup beef stock
Salt and freshly ground black pepper
Bouquet garni
$\frac{1}{4}$ lb mushrooms, washed and sliced

To garnish:
2 tablespoons finely chopped parsley

Cooking Time: 1$\frac{1}{4}$–1$\frac{1}{2}$ hours
Oven: 325°F

Marinate the meat in a bowl with the onions, carrots, peppercorns, herbs and half the wine for about 12 hours. Turn over from time to time. Heat the oil and butter in a frying pan and fry the onions and bacon strips until golden brown, remove to a casserole. Drain the meat from the marinade and brown over a fairly high heat in the frying pan. Heat brandy gently and ignite, pour over the meat. Sprinkle the meat with flour, add the crushed garlic then pour over the marinade, remaining wine and stock. When the liquid is simmering pour into the casserole. Add seasoning, bouquet garni and mushrooms and simmer for 1–1$\frac{1}{4}$ hours. Taste and adjust seasoning. Remove meat to a serving dish with onions and mushrooms. Remove the bay leaf and bouquet garni. Reduce the gravy slightly and strain over the meat. Sprinkle with chopped parsley.

Italian beef casserole; Burgundian beef

New England boiled dinner

2 tablespoons oil
2 onions, peeled and sliced
2 carrots, peeled and sliced
1 turnip, peeled and sliced
1 leek, washed and sliced
3½ lbs rolled rump
Bouquet garni
2½ cups beef stock
Salt and freshly ground black pepper
8 medium-sized potatoes, peeled
8 small carrots, peeled
1 small white cabbage, washed and cut into 8 wedges

Cooking Time: 2 hours
Oven: 325°F

Heat the oil in a large casserole and sauté the sliced vegetables, push to the side and brown the meat on all sides. Add bouquet garni, stock and seasoning. Cover and cook in the oven for 1 hour. Add potatoes and carrots, baste well with the liquid, cover and cook for a further 40 minutes. Lastly add the cabbage and cook for a further 15 minutes. Taste and adjust seasoning, remove bouquet garni. Serve on a heated dish surrounded by whole vegetables. The casseroled vegetables may be served with the meat also. Serves 6.

Yorkshire casserole

2 tablespoons oil
2 onions, peeled and diced
1 carrot, washed and sliced
1 leek, washed and sliced
3 sticks celery, washed and sliced
3½ lbs top round
2½ cups beef stock
Bouquet garni
Salt and freshly ground black pepper
1 teaspoon Worcestershire sauce

Cooking Time: 1½ hours
Oven: 375°F then raise to 425°F

Heat the oil and sauté the sliced vegetables in a large casserole, push to the side and brown the meat on all sides, pour in the stock, bouquet garni, seasonings and Worcestershire sauce. Cook, covered for 1 hour. Taste and adjust seasoning. Remove bouquet garni. Slice the beef and serve with the vegetables from the casserole, accompanied by gravy and horseradish sauce with Yorkshire pudding. Serves 6.

New England boiled dinner; Yorkshire puddings; Yorkshire casserole

Yorkshire pudding

1 cup flour
½ teaspoon salt
2 eggs
1¼ cups milk
2 tablespoons cooking fat

Cooking Time: small 15 minutes, large 30–45 minutes
Oven: 425°F

Make up the batter by sifting the flour and salt into a bowl. Make a well in the center of the flour, drop in the beaten eggs and half the milk. Mix thoroughly, beating so that all the flour is absorbed gradually and until mixture is thick, smooth and creamy. Lightly beat in the milk and use as required.

For puddings heat the fat in muffin tins or a suitable size baking dish until it is very hot, then pour in the batter. Bake on the top shelf of the oven until well risen and golden brown.

27

Bolognese sauce

2 tablespoons oil
1 thick slice bacon, finely chopped
2 onions, peeled and finely diced
1 clove garlic, crushed
1 small carrot, peeled and diced
1 stalk celery, washed and thinly sliced
1 lb ground beef
2 oz chicken livers, finely chopped
16 oz can tomatoes
2 tablespoons tomato paste
1 bay leaf
1 teaspoon oregano
2 tablespoons red wine
$\frac{2}{3}$ cup chicken stock
Salt and freshly ground black pepper

Cooking Time: 1–1$\frac{1}{4}$ hours
Oven: 350°F

Heat the oil in a frying pan. Fry the bacon until golden. Add onions, garlic, carrot, and celery and allow to cook gently for 4 minutes, then remove to a casserole. Brown the beef on a brisk heat, then add the chicken livers and allow to brown, add tomatoes, allow to heat through and pour into a casserole. Mix the paste, herbs and wine with the stock, pour into the frying pan to heat and remove any meat juice which was left behind. Season well, pour over the meat and simmer for 45 minutes on top of the range or for 1 hour in the oven. Taste and adjust seasoning. Remove bay leaf. Serve with $\frac{1}{2}$–$\frac{3}{4}$ lb of cooked spaghetti which has been boiled in plenty of salted boiling water for 10 minutes. Drain well then toss in a little butter, with a little freshly ground pepper and a little nutmeg. Serve with grated cheese.

Béchamel sauce

2$\frac{1}{2}$ cups milk
1 small carrot, peeled and sliced
1 onion, peeled, quartered and stuck
with 4 cloves
6 peppercorns
1 bay leaf
4 tablespoons butter
7 tablespoons flour
Salt and freshly ground black pepper

Cooking Time: 35 minutes

Place the milk in a saucepan with the carrot, onion, peppercorns and bay leaf. Heat the milk on a very low heat until just under boiling, simmer for a few minutes then cover and allow to stand for 15–30 minutes. Strain the milk; melt the butter in a clean saucepan, add the flour and beat well until a roux is formed, gradually whisk or beat in the milk over a low heat until a smooth sauce is obtained, taste and adjust the seasoning.

Cannelloni

8 cannelloni
$\frac{1}{2}$ quantity Bolognese sauce
1 teaspoon oil
2$\frac{1}{2}$ cups Béchamel sauce
Salt and freshly ground black pepper
2 tablespoons light cream
$\frac{1}{2}$ cup grated cheese

Cooking Time: 45 minutes
Oven: 350°F

Boil the cannelloni in plenty of boiling salted water until barely tender. Stuff the tubes of cannelloni with Bolognese sauce and arrange in an oiled casserole dish. Pour on the Béchamel sauce and season well. Cover and cook in the oven for 30 minutes. Sprinkle with cream and grated cheese and return to the oven, uncovered, for 15 minutes. Place under the grill to brown the top, if preferred.

Variation

Some people may prefer the more traditional Italian cannelloni stuffed with spinach and ricotta cheese and topped with a Béchamel sauce.

Canneloni with Béchamel sauce; Spaghetti with Bolognese sauce

Lamb is available to us all the year round. It makes delicious casseroles as long, slow cooking is ideal for the less tender cuts. However lamb tends to have lots of fat so it is best to skim after cooking.
Suitable cuts for the casserole: Shoulder, Breast, Neck and Short ribs.

Australian fruit casserole

8 small lamb chops
1 tablespoon butter
1 clove garlic, crushed
1 small onion, peeled and diced
1 tablespoon honey
½ teaspoon dry mustard
1 small apple, diced
1 small piece root ginger, chopped
2 tablespoons dark raisins
⅔ cup chicken stock
1 teaspoon cornstarch
Salt and freshly ground black pepper

To garnish:
1 red apple, sliced
1 tablespoon lemon juice

Cooking Time: 40 minutes
Oven: 350°F

Broil the chops under a preheated broiler for 2 minutes each side to brown and remove fat. Heat the butter in a casserole, add garlic and onion and cook for 3–4 minutes on a low heat. Add the honey and mustard, remove from the heat and coat chops in the honey and onion mixture. Arrange in the casserole, add apple, ginger and raisins. Mix the stock with the cornstarch, season well, bring to the boil and pour over the chops. Cook in the oven for 30 minutes, taste and adjust the seasoning. Garnish with a sliced red apple which has been dipped in lemon juice.

Braised chops in mint jelly

8 loin lamb chops, boned and rolled
1 large onion, peeled and sliced
Few mint leaves
Salt and freshly ground black pepper
1¼ cups veal stock or water

Jelly:
1¼ cups stock from the chops
A good bunch of fresh mint leaves, washed and chopped
5 tablespoons wine vinegar
5 teaspoons gelatin
4 tablespoons very hot water

To garnish:
Mint sprigs (optional)

Cooking Time: 50 minutes
Oven: 325°F

Fry the chops in a casserole to brown on each side, without fat. Add the onion, the mint leaves, seasoning and stock. Bring to the boil, cover and cook in the oven for 40 minutes. Remove the chops, cool and place on a serving dish in the refrigerator. Cool the stock from the chops and skim away the fat. Add the mint and wine vinegar. Dissolve the gelatin thoroughly by sprinkling in hot water, add to the mint liquid and pour over rolled chops. Allow to set, garnish with mint leaves, if liked and serve with salad and new potatoes.

Australian fruit casserole; Braised chops in mint jelly

Braised loin of lamb

Salt and freshly ground black pepper
1 loin of lamb, boned, rolled and tied
1 tablespoon oil
2 tablespoons butter
½ lb haricot beans, soaked
2 large carrots, peeled and diced
1 turnip, peeled and diced
1 bay leaf
1¼ cups veal or white stock
2 tablespoons butter
3 tablespoons flour

To garnish:
4 tomatoes, skinned
Parsley

Cooking Time: 1¾ hours
Oven: 350°F

Season meat well with salt and pepper. Brown meat on all sides in the oil and melted butter in a casserole. Remove meat. Fry the vegetables quickly in hot fat. Replace meat on top of vegetables in the casserole, add the bay leaf and stock and cover the pan. Cook gently in the oven for 1½ hours. Taste and adjust the seasoning. Remove the bay leaf. Remove meat, serve on dish surrounded by strained vegetables. Garnish with tomatoes and parsley. Make a sauce with butter, flour, and strained vegetable stock. Taste and adjust seasoning and serve in a heated sauce boat.

Indian lamb

1½ lbs shoulder of lamb, boned and cut
into 1 inch cubes
½ teaspoon ground coriander
½ teaspoon cardamom
½ teaspoon poppy seeds
½ teaspoon ground cinnamon
¼ teaspoon ground cloves
½ teaspoon salt
½ teaspoon ground black pepper
2 inch piece stem ginger, finely chopped
2 cloves garlic, crushed
1¼ cups plain natural yogurt
1 tablespoon butter
1 large onion, peeled and finely sliced
¼ cup sliced flaked almonds

To garnish:
Chopped parsley
1 large tomato, peeled and
sliced (optional)
1 small onion, peeled and sliced into
rings (optional)

Cooking Time: 1¼ hours
Oven: 325°F

Place the lamb in a bowl with the coriander, cardamom, poppy seeds, cinnamon, cloves, salt and pepper, ginger and garlic. Mix well then add the yogurt. Leave lamb to marinate in this mixture for several hours, in a casserole. Heat the butter, fry the sliced onion until just beginning to brown, do not burn, add the almonds. Transfer to a plate. Remove meat from the marinade and brown, return to casserole. Add the remaining marinade to the frying pan, stir well and pour over the meat in the casserole. Rinse out frying pan with a little water to obtain all juices, add to the casserole with fried onion rings and almonds. Cover and cook in the oven for 1 hour or until the meat is tender. Serve on a bed of saffron rice and garnish with chopped parsley. Alternatively, the dish may be garnished with tomato slices and onion rings.

Braised loin of lamb; Indian lamb; Casseroled loin chops

Casseroled loin chops

2 onions, peeled and sliced
2 teaspoons oil
¼ teaspoon cinnamon
¼ teaspoon cloves
1 clove garlic, crushed
½ lb tomatoes, skinned and sliced
Salt and freshly ground black pepper
4 lamb chops
Watercress sprigs to garnish

Cooking Time: 1 hour
Oven: 325°F

Fry the onions in the oil in a frying pan until golden brown. Add the spices, garlic, tomatoes and seasoning. Cook for a few minutes, add the chops. Transfer to a casserole, and cook in the oven for 45 minutes–1 hour. Garnish with watercress sprigs before serving.

33

Lamb and eggplant casserole

4 medium-sized eggplants, washed
1 tablespoon oil
1 lb ground lamb
1 large onion, peeled and finely diced
1 clove garlic, crushed (optional)
2 tablespoons finely chopped parsley
½ teaspoon dried rosemary
Salt and freshly ground black pepper
29 oz can tomatoes
½ teaspoon Worcestershire sauce

Cooking Time: 40 minutes
Oven: 350°F

Cut the eggplants in half lengthwise and scoop out the central core leaving a fairly thick shell. Blanch the halves for 1 minute in boiling water, then arrange in a casserole. Dice the remaining flesh. Heat the oil in a frying pan, add the ground lamb and brown lightly over a high heat. Add the eggplants, onion and garlic and turn down the heat. Stir frequently until onion becomes opaque. Add the parsley, rosemary and seasoning, mix well and remove from heat. Fill eggplant halves with lamb mixture. Purée the tomatoes through a sieve or in a blender, season well, add Worcestershire sauce and pour over eggplants. Cover the casserole and cook. Taste and adjust seasoning.

Tarragon lamb; Irish stew

Lamb and eggplant casserole

Irish stew

2 large onions, peeled and sliced
2 lbs neck of lamb, cut into slices
2 teaspoons mixed dried parsley, thyme,
basil (optional)
Salt and freshly ground black pepper
2–3 large potatoes, peeled and sliced
2½ cups veal stock or water

To garnish:
1 tablespoon finely chopped parsley

Cooking Time: 1½ hours
Oven: 350°F

Place some sliced onion in a casserole, with the lamb on top.
Sprinkle with herbs, if desired, season well. Add remaining onions
and sliced potatoes mixed, season well, pour in stock. Place in the
oven, covered, for 1¼ hours. Uncover for remaining 15 minutes, to
allow the top to brown slightly. Serve sprinkled with freshly chopped
parsley and colorful vegetables such as peas and carrots. It is most
important that this dish is seasoned well.

Tarragon lamb

5 tablespoons butter
2 lb leg of lamb
2 cups veal or white stock
⅔ cup dry white wine
1 bouquet fresh tarragon
Salt and freshly ground black pepper
1 tablespoon and 1 teaspoon cornstarch
2 tablespoons of cream (optional)

Cooking Time: 1–1¼ hours
Oven: 350°F

Heat 3 tablespoons of the butter in a casserole and sear the leg of
lamb on all sides. Add the remainder of the butter, the stock and
wine and cook for 45 minutes. Remove the meat and reduce the
liquid by half. Add the tarragon and seasoning. Thicken with the
cornstarch and add the cream, if used. Taste and adjust the seasoning, remove the tarragon. Slice the lamb and serve with sauce
poured over.

Lamb with dill sauce

1½ lb leg or shoulder of lamb cut into
1 inch cubes
2 teaspoons salt
5–6 peppercorns
Bunch of dill
2 carrots, peeled and thinly sliced
2 onions, peeled and thinly sliced
2 parsnips, peeled and thinly sliced
4 tablespoons butter
7 tablespoons flour
2½ cups veal or white stock
2 tablespoons white vinegar
1 tablespoon sugar
Salt and freshly ground black pepper
1 egg yolk
3 tablespoons heavy cream

To garnish:
Dill sprigs (optional)

Cooking Time: 1¼ hours approx.
Oven: 325°F

Place the meat in a large casserole, cover with water, bring to the boil. Remove any scum. Add salt, peppercorns and the bunch of dill stalks. Cook over a slow heat until tender, or in the oven. Add the carrots, onions and parsnips and continue cooking for 20–30 minutes until vegetables are just cooked. Drain the meat and vegetables and reserve the stock. Keep the meat and vegetables warm. Melt the butter in a saucepan. Add the flour. Cook for a few minutes but do not brown. Add the stock, stirring constantly until the sauce is smooth and thick. Add the vinegar and sugar and season to taste. Mix the egg yolk with the cream in a small bowl. Add this to the sauce beating constantly, simmer gently for 4–5 minutes, but do not boil. Add the meat and 2–3 tablespoons finely chopped dill. Taste and adjust the seasoning. Serve with the chopped vegetables. Garnish with a few sprigs of dill, if available.

Creamed lamb with cucumber

2 lbs lean cooked lamb, diced
3 scallions or 1 small onion, finely sliced
1½ teaspoons salt
Freshly ground black pepper
1 egg
1 cucumber, washed
¼ teaspoon nutmeg
¼ teaspoon basil
Good pinch dill
Mint
2 tablespoons butter
2 tablespoons cider vinegar
4 tablespoons butter
7 tablespoons flour
2½ cups milk
1 teaspoon lemon juice

To garnish:
Bacon slices
Parsley (optional)

Cooking Time: 50 minutes
Oven: 350°F

Combine lamb and onions, season well. Hard boil the egg. Cut the cucumber in half lengthwise. Remove the seeds, cut into 1 inch slices. Season with nutmeg, basil, dill and a little chopped mint. Heat the butter in a casserole. Add cucumber, salt and vinegar, cover and simmer gently for 10 minutes. Remove cover and slightly increase heat to a rapid boil to reduce the liquid a little. The cucumber should then be tender, but not brown. Reduce heat, stir in the lamb, heat gently in the oven for 20 minutes. Prepare sauce by making a roux with the butter and flour, then adding milk and stirring over a low heat until the mixture thickens. Add chopped egg and lemon juice to the sauce. Combine the lamb and cucumber with the sauce and simmer gently for 20 minutes. Taste and adjust the seasoning. Garnish with grilled bacon rolls and parsley, if liked and serve with sautéed potatoes.

Lamb with dill sauce; Creamed lamb with cucumber; Lamb chops rosemary

Lamb chops rosemary

1 tablespoon Dijon mustard
1 teaspoon soy sauce
½ teaspoon chopped fresh rosemary or
¼ teaspoon dried
¼ teaspoon dried ginger
1 clove garlic, crushed
Salt and freshly ground black pepper
2 tablespoons white wine
2 tablespoons cider vinegar
4 lamb chops
2 tablespoons water
1 teaspoon cornstarch
2 tablespoons light cream
½ teaspoon brown sugar

To garnish:
Rosemary sprigs

Cooking Time: 40 minutes
Oven: 325°F

Mix the mustard, soy sauce, rosemary, ginger, garlic, seasoning, wine and vinegar together. Spread on the chops and allow to marinate for several hours. Brown chops on both sides without oil. Pour over marinade and water. Cook in the oven for 35 minutes. Taste and adjust seasoning. Thicken the liquid with the cornstarch. Pour on the cream and sprinkle with brown sugar. Return to the oven for 5 minutes and serve garnished with sprigs of rosemary. Delicious with baked potatoes and peas.

Greek shepherd's pie

1 large eggplant, washed and sliced
1 tablespoon lemon juice
4 tablespoons butter
2 onions, peeled and thinly sliced
1 large potato, peeled and thinly sliced
1 lb ground lamb
2 tomatoes, peeled and sliced
½ recipe Béchamel sauce (page 29)
Salt and freshly ground black pepper
½ cup grated cheese

Cooking Time: 1 hour
Oven: 325°F

Arrange the sliced eggplant on a plate, sprinkle with a little salt and lemon juice and allow to stand for 15 minutes. Heat the butter and gently fry the onions first then the eggplant and finally the potato, without breaking the slices, for a few minutes. Remove each batch to a plate as fried. Brown the lamb. Place a layer of eggplant and onion in a casserole, then lamb and tomatoes, a little sauce, and season well. Then layer potatoes, lamb and a little sauce. Finish with eggplant, tomatoes and remaining sauce, sprinkle with grated cheese and cook for 45 minutes.

Leek and lamb casserole; Greek shepherd's pie

Lamb with pineapple

Lamb with pineapple

2 tablespoons butter
2 small onions, peeled and diced
1 tablespoon mild curry powder
1 tablespoon flour
1¼ cups veal stock or water
1¼ cups pineapple juice
1½ lbs stewing lamb, trimmed and cut into
1 inch pieces
1–2 cups canned pineapple pieces
¼ cup dark raisins
1 egg yolk
2 tablespoons milk

To garnish:
1 banana, thinly sliced

Cooking Time: 1½ hours
Oven: 325°F

Heat the butter in a frying pan and sauté the onions over a low heat, then stir in the curry powder and fry for a minute over a high heat, stir until blended, add the flour. Fry until colored slightly, add the stock and stir well, then add drained pineapple juice. Turn into a casserole with the lamb, pineapple pieces, reserving a few for decoration, and raisins. Cover and cook in the oven until lamb is tender. When cooked remove from heat and add some stock to the beaten egg yolk and milk, return to hot casserole and stir until liquid thickens slightly. Taste and adjust seasoning. Serve on a bed of rice with sliced bananas dipped in lemon juice and a few pieces of pineapple.

Leek and lamb casserole

1½ lbs neck of lamb
7 tablespoons flour
1 teaspoon salt
Freshly ground black pepper
2 tablespoons cooking fat
3 leeks, coarsely sliced
16 oz can tomatoes
1¼ cups veal stock or water
1 tablespoon tomato paste
½ teaspoon dried thyme
1 teaspoon rosemary

Cooking Time: 2¼ hours
Oven: 325°F

Toss lamb in flour seasoned with salt and pepper. Melt dripping in a large pan and fry the lamb on all sides to brown. Place in a casserole. Fry leeks gently for 2 minutes and place in the casserole with drained tomatoes, reserving juice. Add remaining flour to fat in the pan and cook for 1 minute. Stir in stock or water, juice from canned tomatoes, tomato paste, mixed herbs and seasoning. Bring to the boil, stirring. Pour over lamb. Cover and cook in a moderate oven for 2 hours. Taste and adjust seasoning before serving.

Old time lamb; Noisettes in redcurrant jelly

Old time lamb

1 large breast of lamb, boned
Salt and freshly ground black pepper
¾ cup breadcrumbs
2 teaspoons finely chopped parsley
1 teaspoon finely chopped chives
1 teaspoon finely chopped mint
1 scallion, washed and chopped
6 canned apricot halves, chopped
1 egg, beaten
2 tablespoons sherry
1¼ cups veal or white stock

To garnish:
Chopped scallion greens
Halved apricots

Cooking Time: 2 hours
Oven: 325°F

Lay out the breast of lamb and season well. Mix breadcrumbs, parsley, chives, mint, scallion, apricots and egg together, season well. Spread on to the lamb and roll up, secure with skewers and brown under a preheated hot broiler for several minutes, then place in a casserole. Pour over the sherry and stock, season well and cook for 2 hours. Add extra water or stock if necessary during cooking. Serve on a heated dish, reduce stock in casserole to a glaze, pour over the lamb and garnish with scallion greens and halved apricots.

Oriental lamb

Noisettes in redcurrant jelly

8 noisettes of lamb (boned loin or rib
chops, rolled and tied)
2 tablespoons vegetable oil
Salt and freshly ground black pepper
6 tablespoons redcurrant jelly
3 tablespoons port

To garnish:
Watercress sprigs

Cooking Time: 1 hour
Oven: 350°F

Brown the noisettes in the casserole for 2–3 minutes each side in the
oil. Season well and place redcurrant jelly on each noisette. Pour
port over the noisettes and cover. Cook for 1 hour in the oven.
Remove and serve garnished with watercress sprigs.

Oriental lamb

1 lb ground lamb
Salt and freshly ground black pepper
$\frac{1}{4}$ teaspoon dried basil
1 large onion, peeled and sliced
2 tablespoons oil
1 leek, washed and sliced
Seasoned flour
1 eggplant, washed and diced
16 oz can tomatoes
1 cinnamon stick
Pinch ground coriander
Few cumin seeds
4 tablespoons water
$\frac{2}{3}$ cup white wine

Cooking Time: $1\frac{1}{4}$ hours
Oven: 325°F

Mix the lamb in a bowl with the seasoning and basil. Make into
small balls. Sauté the onion in oil until tender, add the leek and
leave pan on low heat. Coat the balls of lamb with seasoned flour.
Remove the leek and onion to a casserole. Fry lamb until golden
brown and add to the casserole. Place eggplant, tomatoes, cinnamon,
herbs and spices in the pan with the water and wine. Bring to the
boil and pour over the lamb and cook for one hour in the oven.
Taste and adjust seasoning before serving.

41

Orange lamb casserole

Orange lamb casserole

2 tablespoons oil
2 lbs stewing or shoulder lamb, cut
into cubes
1 teaspoon paprika
1 tablespoon butter
1 large onion, peeled and sliced
$\frac{1}{4}$ lb mushrooms, washed and sliced
$\frac{2}{3}$ cup water
1 teaspoon prepared horseradish
Pinch rosemary
Fresh mint leaves or $\frac{1}{2}$ teaspoon dried
2 fresh leaves sage or $\frac{1}{4}$ teaspoon dried
1 teaspoon salt
Freshly ground black pepper
$\frac{2}{3}$ cup sour cream
Finely grated rind of 1 orange
3 tablespoons orange juice

Cooking Time: $1\frac{1}{4}$ hours
Oven: 350°F

Heat the oil, sprinkle lamb with paprika and brown in the frying pan. Cook until lamb is pale brown on all sides, remove to casserole. Add butter to pan, then sauté onion and mushrooms. Add the water, horseradish, herbs, salt and pepper and pour over lamb. Cover the casserole and cook in the oven for 1 hour or until the lamb is tender. Remove the meat and keep hot, add sour cream to onion mixture with grated orange rind and juice. Heat very gently, replace the meat, taste and adjust seasoning and serve.
Alternatively pour on sour cream before serving and sprinkle with orange juice and grated orange rind.

Lamb hot pot

Lamb hot pot

2 tablespoons oil
2 lbs shoulder lamb chops, cut into
1 inch cubes
2 tablespoons seasoned flour
1 lb onions, peeled and sliced
2 stalks celery, washed and sliced
½ lb carrots, peeled and sliced
1 leek, washed and sliced
1 lb potatoes, peeled and sliced
1¼ cups veal or white stock
1 teaspoon Worcestershire sauce
1 teaspoon finely chopped rosemary
Salt and freshly ground black pepper
1 tablespoon butter

To garnish:
1 tablespoon finely chopped
parsley (optional)

Cooking Time: 2¼ hours
Oven: 350°F

Heat the oil in a frying pan. Coat lamb in seasoned flour and brown in the oil. Add the onions and celery and reduce the heat for 5 minutes. Layer the lamb in a casserole with the onion mixture, carrots and leek, finishing with the potatoes. Pour in stock, Worcestershire sauce and rosemary. Season well. Dot with butter, cover and cook for 1¼ hours. Remove the lid for remaining 45 minutes of cooking time. Garnish with chopped parsley, if liked.

Sweet and sour lamb

1 breast lamb, boned, trimmed and cut
into 1 inch cubes
$\frac{2}{3}$ cup vinegar
$\frac{2}{3}$ cup veal stock or pineapple juice
$\frac{1}{2}$ teaspoon salt
3 tablespoons brown sugar
1 medium-sized onion, sliced
$8\frac{1}{4}$ oz can pineapple chunks
Scant 2 tablespoons arrowroot

Cooking Time: $2\frac{1}{4}$ hours
Oven: 350°F

Fry the lamb gently for 3–4 minutes. Place in a casserole, combine the other ingredients, except the arrowroot, and pour over the lamb. Bake in a moderate oven for 2 hours until tender. When cooked, skim off the fat and thicken sauce with arrowroot. Taste and adjust the seasoning and serve with fried rice.

Lemon lamb casserole; Honeyed lamb

Sweet and sour lamb

Lemon lamb casserole

1 lb ground lamb
1 onion, peeled and finely chopped
1 potato, peeled and grated
1 egg
Salt and freshly ground black pepper
1 tablespoon finely chopped parsley
3 tablespoons flour
2 tablespoons butter
$\frac{2}{3}$ cup chicken stock
Finely grated rind of 1 lemon
2 tablespoons lemon juice
2 eggs beaten
Lemon wedges and parsley sprigs to garnish

Cooking Time: 45 minutes
Oven: 350°F

Put the ground lamb, onion, grated potato, egg, seasoning and parsley into a bowl and mix well. Form into small balls, roll in flour and allow to firm in the refrigerator. Heat the butter in a casserole and fry the floured lamb until golden brown. Pour in the stock, add lemon rind and juice, bring to the boil and cook in the oven for 30 minutes. Remove the lamb to a heated serving dish. Add the stock slowly and carefully to the beaten eggs and return to a very low heat to thicken. The mixture must not boil. Taste and adjust the seasoning and pour the egg mixture over the lamb. Garnish with lemon wedges and parsley sprigs.

Honeyed lamb

2 tablespoons oil
2 potatoes, peeled and sliced
1 large onion, peeled and sliced
2 stalks celery, washed and sliced
2 lb breast of lamb, boned, rolled and tied
Salt and freshly ground black pepper
2 teaspoons flour
1 orange
2 tablespoons honey
$1\frac{1}{4}$ cups chicken stock

Cooking Time: $1\frac{3}{4}$ hours
Oven: 350°F

Heat oil and sauté the vegetables for a few minutes and transfer to a casserole. Sprinkle breast of lamb with seasoning and flour and brown on all sides, place in casserole. Cut the orange in half and squeeze the juice from one half and grate a little rind from the squeezed skin. Mix the juice and rind with the honey, add the stock and pour over the breast of lamb. Season well and cover, cook in the oven for $1\frac{1}{2}$ hours. Serve breast cut into slices garnished with orange wedges and vegetables.

Leg of lamb, French style

$3\frac{1}{2}$ lb leg of lamb
2 cloves garlic, peeled and thinly sliced
8 rosemary sprigs
1 medium-sized onion, peeled and sliced
$\frac{2}{3}$ cup red wine
$\frac{2}{3}$ cup veal or white stock
Salt and freshly ground black pepper
8 small potatoes, peeled
8 small carrots, peeled
1 tablespoon flour

Cooking Time: $1\frac{1}{2}$ hours
Oven: 350°F

Make small slits in the leg of lamb. Insert slices of garlic into slits, alternating with small sprigs of fresh rosemary. Arrange onion on the bottom of the casserole, place lamb on top. Pour on the wine and stock, season well, cover and put in the oven for 35 minutes. Cook the potatoes and carrots in boiling salted water for 5 minutes. Drain and sprinkle with salt and pepper, add to casserole, cook for a further 35 minutes. Remove lid of casserole for remaining 15 minutes to allow meat to brown. Serve on a platter surrounded by vegetables. Pour off excess fat, if any, from gravy. Reduce on a high heat and sprinkle in flour, stir well to thicken slightly. Serve in a sauceboat separately.

Spiced Persian lamb

1 lb boneless shoulder of lamb, cut into
1 inch cubes
$\frac{3}{4}$ cup plain yogurt
4 cloves
4 black peppercorns
2 small sticks cinnamon
1 teaspoon turmeric
4 large onions, finely sliced
$\frac{1}{4}$ lb butter
$\frac{1}{2}$ teaspoon paprika
$\frac{1}{2}$ teaspoon chilli powder
$\frac{1}{2}$ teaspoon curry powder
Pinch ground nutmeg
Pinch ground cloves
3–4 cumin seeds (optional)
2–3 cardamoms (optional)
16 oz can tomatoes
$1\frac{1}{4}$ cups veal or white stock
2 potatoes, peeled and diced
Salt

To garnish:
Chopped parsley
Tomato wedges

Cooking Time: $1\frac{1}{2}$ hours

Place the meat in a mixing bowl with the yogurt, 2 cloves, 2 peppercorns, one piece of cinnamon and half the turmeric. Mix well and leave for at least 2 hours. Fry the onions in the butter until golden brown. Add the remaining spices and fry for a few minutes. Add the meat and cook, stirring, over a moderate heat for 5 minutes. Add the tomatoes, stock and potatoes and stir well. Cover and simmer for $1–1\frac{1}{4}$ hours, until the lamb is tender. Taste and adjust seasoning and serve with boiled rice. Garnish, if liked, with tomato wedges and chopped parsley.

As pork animals are usually young, most cuts are tender and can be cooked by any method. Less time is therefore required for pork casseroles to tenderize the meat than for beef and lamb stewing cuts. Ham and pork casseroles can add variety to everyday menus and ham is especially good to add flavor to veal casseroles. A slice or two of bacon is often used to flavor other meat and poultry casseroles. Choose pork with firm, smooth flesh without gristle and a light marbling of fat. Flesh should never be gray and soft. Good quality animals have a thick layer of fat on the outside.

Hock and pea lunch casserole; Casseroled sausages; Cranberry pork

Hock and pea lunch casserole

1 tablespoon oil
1 onion, peeled and sliced
2 lbs smoked hock, trimmed and cubed
11½ oz can split pea with ham soup
diluted with ¼ cup water
Freshly ground pepper
2 potatoes, peeled and diced
Sprig of thyme or ¼ teaspoon dried
½ box frozen peas

To garnish:
Triangles of toast (optional)
Mint leaves (optional)

Cooking Time: 1¾ hours
Oven: 350°F

Heat oil, sauté the onion gently for 2 minutes, then add the cubed hock and cook for 3–4 minutes. Place the hock and onion in a casserole with the diluted split pea and ham soup, pepper, potatoes and thyme. Cover and cook in the oven for 1½ hours. Stir in the peas 15 minutes before cooking has finished. Taste and adjust seasoning. Garnish with triangles of toast and mint leaves if liked.

Cranberry pork

2 tablespoons oil
3½ lb rolled shoulder of pork
½ lb cranberries
⅔ cup water
Salt and freshly ground black pepper
2 tablespoons honey
1 teaspoon finely grated orange rind
Pinch of ground cloves
Pinch of ground nutmeg

Cooking Time: 1¾ hours
Oven: 350°F

Heat the oil and brown the pork in a frying pan on all sides. Cook the cranberries for 5 minutes in the water after it has boiled. Transfer the pork to the casserole, season well and spread with the honey and grated orange rind. Sprinkle with cloves and nutmeg, pour in the cranberries and cook in the oven for 1½ hours. Taste and adjust seasoning. Serve sliced with the sauce.

Casseroled sausages

4 large pork sausages with herbs
4 thick slices bacon
1 onion, peeled and chopped
1 tablespoon butter
2 tablespoons oil
1½ teaspoons dried sage
1 tablespoon flour
2 cups veal or white stock
Salt and freshly ground black pepper
⅔ cup sour cream
8 oz noodles
2 tablespoons butter
Pinch nutmeg

To garnish:
2 tablespoons finely chopped parsley

Cooking Time: 40 minutes

Roll up each sausage in a slice of bacon, and tie round with fine string to secure. Fry the onion gently in the butter and oil for 5 minutes. Add the sage and the tied sausages and fry for 5 minutes. Remove the sausages to a plate. Stir the flour into the fat remaining in the pan and cook for 1 minute. Gradually stir in the stock. Bring to the boil and add the seasoning and sour cream. Return the sausages and stock to the casserole. Simmer for 20 minutes, taste and adjust the seasoning. Cook the noodles in a large saucepan of boiling salted water for about 8 minutes. Drain and toss in butter with a pinch of nutmeg and pepper. Serve sausages with cooked noodles, sprinkled with chopped parsley.

Honeyed shoulder of pork with red cabbage

2 tablespoons oil
3 lb shoulder of pork
1 tablespoon butter
2 small onions, peeled and sliced
1 small red cabbage, washed
and shredded
$\frac{2}{3}$ cup red wine
$\frac{2}{3}$ cup stock
Salt and freshly ground black pepper
2 tablespoons honey

Cooking Time: $1\frac{1}{2}$–$1\frac{3}{4}$ hours
Oven: 350°F

Heat the oil in a frying pan and brown the pork on all sides. Remove from pan. Add the butter and sauté the onions, transfer to a casserole. Blanch the cabbage by placing it in boiling water for about 3 minutes. Drain well and place in the casserole with the onions. Pour over the red wine and stock and season well. Spread the honey over the skin of the pork and place on the vegetable mixture. Cover and cook in the oven for $1\frac{1}{2}$ hours. Taste and adjust seasoning.

Hawaiian pork casserole

1 lb pork, cubed
$15\frac{1}{4}$ oz can pineapple chunks
Salt and freshly ground black pepper
$\frac{1}{2}$ teaspoon allspice
3 tablespoons oil
1 onion, peeled and finely chopped
1 green pepper, seeded and sliced
3 tablespoons seasoned flour
$\frac{2}{3}$ cup veal or white stock
1 tablespoon sherry
1 tablespoon cornstarch

To garnish:
Rings of green pepper

Cooking Time: 1 hour
Oven: 325°F

Marinate the pork in the pineapple juice with seasoning and allspice for 1 hour. Heat 1 tablespoon of the oil and sauté the onion and green pepper for 5 minutes. Transfer the vegetables to a casserole. Drain the pork, dip in seasoned flour and fry in the remaining oil until golden brown. Place in the casserole with the marinade, stock and sherry. Cover and put in the oven to cook. After 45 minutes thicken the gravy with the cornstarch and add the pineapple chunks. Taste and adjust the seasoning. Serve garnished with rings of raw green pepper.

Spanish pork chops

4 thick slices bacon, chopped
1 tablespoon oil
1 onion, peeled and chopped
4 pork chops, with kidneys
1 tablespoon seasoned flour
$\frac{2}{3}$ cup red wine
1 tablespoon tomato paste
20 stuffed olives, sliced

To garnish:
2 hard-boiled eggs, sliced

Cooking Time: 35 minutes
Oven: 375°F

Fry the bacon, remove to a casserole, add oil to frying pan. Sauté onion for a few minutes and transfer to the casserole. Dust the chops with seasoned flour and fry on both sides to brown and place in the casserole on the bacon and onion. Mix the wine with the tomato paste and pour over the chops. Cook in the oven for 25 minutes then add the olives and cook for an additional 5 minutes. Garnish with slices of hard-boiled egg with a slice of olive in the center.

Sweet and sour pork

1 tablespoon oil
1 tablespoon sherry
1 tablespoon honey
2 tablespoons vinegar
1 tablespoon soy sauce
Salt and freshly ground black pepper
1 lb pork, cubed
2 tablespoons oil
1 onion, peeled and diced
2 carrots, peeled and diced
1 green pepper, seeded and diced
5 mushrooms, washed and sliced
1¼ cups veal or white stock
1 tablespoon soy sauce
1¼ cups canned bean sprouts, drained
1 tablespoon cornstarch

Cooking Time: 1 hour
Oven: 325°F

Mix the oil, sherry, honey, vinegar and soy sauce in a bowl and season well. Marinate the pork in the mixture for at least 2 hours, turning from time to time. Heat 1 tablespoon oil and fry the onion, carrots, pepper and mushrooms. Place in a casserole. Drain the pork and brown in the remaining oil. Transfer to the casserole and add the marinade, stock, seasoning and remaining soy sauce. Cover and cook in the oven for 30 minutes, then add the bean sprouts. After 15 minutes thicken the liquid with cornstarch and return to cook for the remaining 15 minutes. Taste and adjust the seasoning.

Lemon and lime pork

2 tablespoons butter
1 clove garlic, peeled and crushed
2 onions, peeled and chopped
1 lb leg of pork, cut into ½ inch pieces
Finely grated rind of 1 lemon
2 tablespoons lime juice
⅔ cup water
2 tablespoons light cream
1 egg yolk
Salt and freshly ground black pepper

To garnish:
Lemon or lime slices

Cooking Time: 1 hour
Oven: 375°F

Heat the butter, add garlic and onions and sauté for a few minutes, transfer to a small casserole. Fry the pork for about 3 minutes, add to the casserole with grated lemon rind, lime juice and water, and cook in the oven for 40 minutes. Place pork in a heated dish. Mix the cream and the egg, season well and pour in some of the lime juice mixture, beat well, add remaining liquid, return to heat until sauce thickens. Taste and adjust the seasoning. Garnish with slices of lime or lemon. Serve with mashed potatoes.

Sweet and sour pork; Lemon and lime pork

Spare ribs

3 lbs Chinese-style spare ribs
4 tablespoons soy sauce
2 tablespoons orange marmalade
1 clove garlic, crushed
1 large onion, peeled and sliced
Salt and freshly ground black pepper
1¼ cups veal stock or water
1 tablespoon vinegar

Cooking Time: 1¾ hours
Oven: 400°F

Brown the spare ribs under a hot broiler. Mix the soy sauce, marmalade, and crushed garlic together and spread over the ribs. Place sliced onion on the bottom of a casserole, place ribs on top, season well. Pour over stock and vinegar. Cover and cook in the oven for 1½ hours. Remove lid to allow to crisp before serving. Taste and adjust the seasoning.

Pork fillet veronique; Stuffed pork chops

Spare ribs

Stuffed pork chops

4 thick pork chops
⅓ cup breadcrumbs
1 teaspoon dried sage
1 small onion, peeled and finely chopped
¼ cup golden raisins
Finely grated rind of ½ lemon
1 egg, beaten
Salt and freshly ground black pepper
1¼ cups cider

To garnish:
1 tablespoon finely chopped parsley
Watercress sprigs
Tomato slices

Cooking Time: 1 hour
Oven: 350°F

Cut a slit in the skin of each chop to allow a pocket for stuffing. Brown the chops on each side quickly under a preheated broiler. Mix the breadcrumbs, sage, onion, raisins and lemon rind in a bowl with the egg, season well. Stuff into the pockets of the chops, arrange in a casserole, season well. Pour over the cider and cook in the oven. Serve on a heated dish, garnished with chopped parsley. Cider sauce may be thickened with cornstarch and served separately. Alternatively, eight thin chops may be used. Sandwich two chops with stuffing between and secure with a wooden tooth pick. Serve on a hot dish, garnished with chopped parsley, watercress sprigs and tomato slices.

Pork fillet veronique

2 pork fillets, trimmed
24 green grapes, halved and seeded
4 tablespoons butter
⅔ cup white wine
⅔ cup chicken stock
Salt and freshly ground black pepper
1 onion, peeled and quartered
1 carrot, peeled and sliced
1 bay leaf
¼ teaspoon or sprig of thyme
2 tablespoons butter
3 tablespoons flour
1 egg yolk
Chopped parsley to garnish

Cooking Time: 1¼ hours
Oven: 350°F

Cut the pork fillets halfway through and open out. Stuff 12 halved grapes with bits of butter and arrange down the center of one fillet, place the other on top to form a roll and tie with string. Heat the remaining butter and brown fillet on all sides, transfer to a casserole, add wine, stock, seasoning, onion and carrot, bay leaf and thyme. Cover and cook for 1 hour. Place pork on a heated serving plate, remove string. Heat the butter until it is slightly brown and quickly add the flour, cook roux until blond, add strained liquid from the casserole. Mix the beaten egg yolk with a little sauce then return to remainder of sauce on a low heat to thicken, taste and adjust seasoning. Pour over fillets, decorate with remaining halved grapes and garnish with chopped parsley.

Ham steaks with pineapple

4 ham steaks
16 cloves
4 teaspoons brown sugar
Freshly ground black pepper
15¼ oz can pineapple rings
2 tomatoes, halved
1 tablespoon cornstarch

Cooking Time: 50 minutes
Oven: 350°F

Snip ham fat with scissors to avoid shrinking, stick cloves into the steaks, sprinkle with brown sugar, and pepper. Pour over the pineapple juice and bake for 40 minutes in a casserole. Uncover, pour off the juice, place a pineapple ring on each steak, top with a halved tomato and replace in the oven to heat through. Thicken the juice by adding cornstarch mixed in a little water, taste and adjust the seasoning and pour over pineapple and ham. Serve with mashed potatoes.

Mediterranean pork

4 pork chops, thinly cut
3 tablespoons flour
Salt and freshly ground black pepper
1 tablespoon oil
4 oz can mushrooms or ¼ lb fresh mushrooms, cooked in water and liquid retained
3 tablespoons tomato paste
1 small onion, peeled and sliced
½ green pepper, seeded and sliced
1 clove garlic, crushed

Cooking Time: 1 hour
Oven: 325°F

Dip the chops in flour seasoned with salt and pepper. Brown quickly, on both sides in the oil. Place the liquid from the mushrooms in the bowl of an electric blender, along with the tomato paste, onion, pepper and garlic and blend for 20 seconds. Pour half into a casserole and add the pork chops and mushrooms, then the remaining tomato mixture. Cover and bake for 40 minutes. Uncover and continue cooking for another 20 minutes.

Braised ham

2¼ lb ham
1¼ cups pale ale
Freshly ground black pepper
2 tablespoons honey
¼ cup dark brown sugar
1 teaspoon dry mustard
12 cloves
Watercress sprigs to garnish

Cooking Time: 1 hour 10 minutes
Oven: 350°F then raise to 400°F

Place the ham in a casserole with pale ale and cook, sprinkled with pepper and covered, for 40 minutes. Remove and discard half the ale. Remove the skin and score the fat diagonally with a sharp knife. Mix honey, sugar and dry mustard together and rub over the ham. Stud diamond shapes on the fat with cloves and return ham to the oven, without lid, and with half the ale, for another 30 minutes at the higher temperature. Baste every 10 minutes.

VEAL

The best veal is milk-fed. The flesh is firm, smooth and a very pale pink. Most of the veal we eat in this country has been partially grass or grain-fed and it is darker in color, from a dark pink at its youngest to a light red as the animal matures into a calf. Choose the palest colored veal available, avoiding any meat that is dark and dry looking. Cuts of veal suitable for the casserole: Shoulder, including the arm, blade and neck, Short Ribs, Shank and Leg.

Veal casserole; Sweet pepper casserole

Veal casserole

2 lbs stewing veal, trimmed and cut into
1 inch cubes
Flour
3 tablespoons oil
4 tablespoons butter
3 medium-sized onions, peeled and cut
into rings
4 thick slices bacon, or $\frac{1}{4}$ lb belly of
pork, cut into $\frac{1}{2}$ inch cubes
$\frac{2}{3}$ cup dry white wine
1 green pepper, seeded and diced
2 carrots, peeled and sliced
16 oz can peeled tomatoes
$\frac{1}{2}$ teaspoon marjoram
$\frac{1}{2}$ teaspoon paprika
Salt and freshly ground black pepper
$\frac{2}{3}$ cup beef stock
$\frac{1}{4}$ lb mushrooms, washed and sliced
$\frac{2}{3}$ cup sour cream

To garnish:
1 tablespoon finely chopped chives
or parsley

Cooking Time: $1\frac{1}{2}$ hours

Dredge the veal with flour and brown in a frying pan in the oil and butter, add onions and sauté until tender, about 5 minutes. Fry bacon or belly of pork until lightly brown, add to the veal and onions. Pour in wine, mix with meat and onions and place in a heavy-based saucepan. Add pepper, carrots and tomatoes. Simmer for 10 minutes. Add herbs, seasoning and stock. Bring to the boil then simmer for 45 minutes. Add sliced mushrooms and simmer for another 20 minutes.
Remove from heat and stir in sour cream. Taste and adjust the seasoning and serve sprinkled with chopped chives or parsley.

Sweet pepper casserole

4 veal chops
1 lb onions, peeled and chopped
4 tablespoons butter
1 tablespoon oil
1 green pepper, seeded and cut into strips
16 oz can tomatoes
$\frac{1}{2}$ teaspoon sugar
1 chicken stock cube
$\frac{2}{3}$ cup boiling water
Salt and freshly ground black pepper
Pinch of marjoram
4 new potatoes, peeled and sliced in rounds

Cooking Time: 40 minutes
Oven: 350°F

Place the chops under a hot broiler for 5 minutes, turning once. Place in a casserole and keep hot. To make the sauce, fry the onions in the butter and oil until transparent. Add the pepper, tomatoes, sugar and the stock cube, dissolved in boiling water, and seasoning. Add to the casserole with the sliced new potatoes and place in a moderate oven for 30 minutes. Taste and adjust the seasoning. Serve with new potatoes and sliced green beans.

Veal rolls

¼ lb chunk bacon
4 tablespoons rendered suet
¾ cup breadcrumbs
Rind of ½ lemon, finely grated
¼ teaspoon dried basil
Salt and freshly ground black pepper
1 egg, beaten
4 thin slices leg of veal
3 tablespoons seasoned flour
¼ cup shortening
2 small onions, peeled and sliced
1 carrot, peeled and sliced
2½ cups stock or water
2 tablespoons tomato paste

To garnish:
Watercress sprigs

Cooking Time: 1¾ hours
Oven: 350°F

Chop the bacon finely, add all the stuffing ingredients and bind with the beaten egg. Pound the veal to flatten with a rolling pin. Spread with the stuffing and roll up and tie with fine string, toss in seasoned flour. Heat the shortening in a casserole, fry meat to brown lightly, drain and remove. Fry sliced onions and carrot and any flour left, for 1–2 minutes. Add the stock or water and tomato paste, taste and adjust the seasoning. Put in veal rolls and cook in the oven for 1½ hours or until meat is tender. Garnish with watercress sprigs before serving.

Veal rolls

Veal paprika

1 lb stewing veal, trimmed of fat
and cubed
1 tablespoon flour
1 tablespoon paprika
Salt and freshly ground black pepper
2 tablespoons margarine
1 onion, peeled and sliced
$\frac{2}{3}$ cup veal stock
2 stalks celery, washed and chopped
$\frac{1}{2}$ lb tomatoes, skinned, seeded
and chopped
1 tablespoon tomato paste
1 tablespoon finely chopped parsley
Paprika
3 tablespoons sour cream

Cooking Time: $1\frac{3}{4}$–2 hours
Oven: 350°F

Toss the veal in flour, paprika and seasoning. Heat margarine gently in a large frying pan. Add the veal and fry with the onion for 5 minutes. Stir in the stock and bring to the boil, stirring, and add celery, tomatoes and tomato paste. Transfer to a casserole. Bake on the middle shelf of the oven for $1\frac{1}{2}$–$1\frac{3}{4}$ hours until meat is tender. Taste and adjust the seasoning. Sprinkle with chopped parsley and paprika, and spoon over sour cream.

Veal paprika

Some Americans prefer the name "variety meats" for these delicious and nutritious parts of the animal. Whether we call them offal or variety meats, they have very little waste and are therefore reasonably economical. Always eat offal fresh and if pre-packed, unwrap and store in the refrigerator until it is to be cooked. Do not store offal in airtight plastic containers. The following offal is suitable for the casserole: Brains, Tongue, Tripe, Pig's head, Heart, Kidneys, Liver and Oxtail.

Lamb kidneys in Cinzano

8 lamb kidneys, cleaned and skinned
½ lb mushrooms, washed
2 teaspoons lemon juice
2 tablespoons butter
Salt and freshly ground black pepper
⅓ cup Cinzano (white)
2 tablespoons cream (optional)

To garnish:
2 tablespoons finely chopped parsley

Cooking Time: 25 minutes
Oven: 325°F

Cut the kidneys in half, remove the core and slice again. Slice the mushrooms lengthwise down the stalks and sprinkle with lemon juice. Heat the butter in a frying pan, sauté the kidneys, then add the mushrooms to cook for about 3 minutes. Season well and arrange in a casserole. Pour over the Cinzano and put in the oven to cook for 20 minutes. Taste and adjust the seasoning. Sprinkle with cream, if liked, and serve garnished with parsley.

Oxtail with sausages

2 oxtails
¼ cup lard
1 large onion, peeled and sliced
2½ cups beef stock
⅔ cup white wine
Bouquet garni
Salt and freshly ground black pepper
4 sausages

Beurre manié
2 tablespoons butter blended with
1 tablespoon flour
1 teaspoon Worcestershire sauce

To garnish:
Parsley sprig

Cooking Time: 3 hours
Oven: 325°F

Brown the oxtails in lard, together with the onion. Drain and transfer to a casserole. Add the stock, white wine, bouquet garni and seasoning. Cook in the oven until tender. Remove the meat from the bones and keep warm. Remove bouquet garni. Skim the fat from the cooled sauce. Cook the sausages until nicely browned and cut each in half. Arrange round the meat on a serving dish. Thicken the sauce with the beurre manié, add the Worcestershire sauce and seasoning, if necessary. Pour over the meat. Garnish with parsley sprig and serve surrounded by a border of mashed potato.

OFFAL
Oxtail casserole

2 oxtails, cut into 2 inch pieces
2 tablespoons oil
2 medium-sized onions, peeled and sliced
2 medium-sized carrots, peeled and sliced
1 clove garlic, crushed
2 tablespoons tomato paste
1¼ cups beef stock
⅔ cup sherry
Salt and freshly ground black pepper
Bouquet garni
1 lb small white onions, peeled
2 tablespoons butter
¼ lb button mushrooms, washed

Cooking Time: 2½ hours
Oven: 325°F

Brown the oxtail in the oil. Remove to a casserole. Sauté the vegetables and put on top of the oxtail. Blend the tomato paste, stock and sherry. Pour over the contents of the casserole. Season and add the bouquet garni. Cook for 2 hours. Remove the bouquet garni. Remove the meat from the bones, if liked and skim the fat from the cooled sauce. Return meat to the casserole and keep warm. Sauté the onions in the butter for 10 minutes, add mushrooms and continue cooking for another 7 minutes. Add to the meat. Simmer together for 10 minutes. Taste and adjust the seasoning before serving.

Potted pig's head

½ pig's head
2¼ quarts cold water
2 onions, peeled and quartered
1 carrot, peeled and halved
1 turnip, peeled and quartered
4 cloves
12 peppercorns
1 blade of mace
Bouquet garni
Salt and freshly ground black pepper

To garnish:
Slices of tomato or hard-boiled egg
Chopped parsley

Cooking Time: 3¼ hours
Oven: 325°F

This recipe is included as it is delicious and some people acquire pigs' heads when buying pork for the freezer. Prepare it in a large casserole to cut down smells in the kitchen. Wash the head thoroughly in tepid water, remove gristle and soft nostrils then rinse thoroughly in cold water. Place the head into a large casserole with enough cold water to cover, bring to the boil slowly. Skim carefully then add the vegetables, spices and bouquet garni. Cover and place in the oven, remove lid and skim after the first and second hours. At the end of 3 hours the flesh should come easily away from the bones. Strain the liquid into a bowl and place head on a dish, allow to cool. Cut tongue and meat from head into pieces, removing all skin, gristle and fat. Place liquid and bones into a pot and boil until it is reduced by half, season well. Place meat in a mold and pour in juice. This will set into a firm jelly and can be turned out on to a bed of salad and garnished with tomato slices or hard-boiled egg and chopped parsley.

Tripe and onions

2½ lbs tripe
1¼ cups milk
1¼ cups water
4 large onions, peeled and thickly sliced
Salt and freshly ground black pepper
2 tablespoons cornstarch

Cooking Time: 2½–3½ hours
Oven: 300°F

Cut the tripe into strips. Bring the milk and water to the boil in a casserole. Add the tripe and onions. Season and simmer gently for 2½ hours or cook in the oven for 3½ hours. Remove. Thicken the sauce with cornstarch and simmer for a few minutes.

Lambs' hearts with celery and apple

1 lb lambs' hearts, washed and
thinly sliced
1 large onion, peeled and sliced
¼ cup lard
6 stalks celery, washed and sliced
1 tablespoon butter
1 tablespoon cornstarch
1¼ cups white or veal stock
1 tablespoon tomato paste
4 tablespoons red wine (optional)
Bouquet garni
Salt and freshly ground black pepper
½ lb apples, washed, cored and sliced

Cooking Time: 2¼ hours
Oven: 325°F

Brown the heart slices and onion in the lard. Place in a casserole. Sauté the celery in the butter. Place in the casserole. Add the cornstarch to the melted butter to make a roux; blend in the stock, paste and red wine and cook well. Add to the casserole with the bouquet garni and seasoning. Arrange sliced apples on top. Cover and cook in the oven for 2 hours. Remove bouquet garni. Taste and adjust the seasoning before serving.

Braised tongue and Madeira

2½–3 lb tongue
1 large onion, peeled and sliced
1 large carrot, peeled and sliced
1 bay leaf
½ teaspoon thyme
6 peppercorns, roughly crushed
Salt and freshly ground black pepper
2 tablespoons butter
3 tablespoons flour
⅔ cup Madeira
Watercress sprigs to garnish

Cooking Time: 3½–3¾ hours
Oven: 300°F

Place the tongue, vegetables, herbs and peppercorns in a saucepan with enough hot water to cover. Bring to the boil, cover with the lid and simmer gently for 3 hours until tender. Remove the tongue, cut away the root and skin. Cut into slices and place in a casserole. Make a brown roux by melting the butter until it is foaming and turns golden on a high heat, add the flour and allow to brown. Add 1¼ cups of cooking liquid and cook until smooth and pale brown. Strain if necessary, add the Madeira and cook for about 2 minutes. Pour over the sliced tongue in the casserole. Cover and cook in the oven for 30 minutes. Serve garnished with watercress sprigs.

Lambs' hearts with celery and apple; Braised tongue and Madeira; Tripe and onions

Stuffed liver casserole

1½ lbs liver (about 6 slices)
3 tablespoons flour

Stuffing:
2 tablespoons breadcrumbs
1 teaspoon finely chopped parsley
½ teaspoon salt
¼ teaspoon freshly ground black pepper
1 onion, peeled and finely chopped
¼ teaspoon grated lemon rind
6–8 thick slices bacon, rinded
1¼ cups veal or white stock
Watercress sprigs to garnish

Cooking Time: 40 minutes
Oven: 375°F

Toss the liver in flour. Mix all the ingredients for the stuffing together, except the bacon and stock, moistening with a little stock. Spread over the liver, wrap each slice with bacon, place in a casserole and pour over the stock so that the liver is covered. Bake about 40 minutes or until the liver is tender. Thicken if necessary with a beurre manié (see page 7) and taste for seasoning before serving. Garnish with watercress sprigs before serving.

Lamb's liver with sherry cream sauce

1 lb lamb's liver cut into slices
2 tablespoons seasoned flour
2 large onions, peeled and sliced
4 tablespoons butter
2 tablespoons cooking sherry
⅔ cup veal or white stock
4 tomatoes, cut into quarters
Salt and freshly ground black pepper
Chopped parsley to garnish

Cooking Time: 40 minutes
Oven: 350°F

Dip the liver in the seasoned flour. Sweat the onions in the melted butter, transfer to a casserole. Add the liver to the frying pan, fry quickly and place in the casserole. Add extra flour if necessary to absorb excess fat. Add the sherry, stock and tomatoes. Bring to the boil stirring, add to liver in casserole, season well and cook for 30 minutes. Garnish with chopped parsley and serve with mashed potatoes or rice.

Today we have an excellent supply of chickens, turkeys and ducks throughout the year because of modern methods of production and freezing. All poultry can be used in casseroles and it is an excellent way of giving flavor to frozen birds. However all frozen poultry should be thawed before cooking.

The carcass is an added bonus as excellent stock can be made from giblets and bones so that nothing is wasted.

To make stock: Place the carcass and giblets in a saucepan with 6 cups of water, 2 onions, peeled and sliced, 2 carrots, peeled and sliced, 2 stalks of celery washed and sliced, 1 bouquet garni, $\frac{1}{4}$ teaspoon salt, 12 peppercorns and bring to the boil. Simmer for 1 hour. Stock can be made in a pressure cooker by following manufacturer's directions.

Chilli chicken casserole

1 tablespoon oil
Salt and freshly ground black pepper
4 chicken drumsticks
2 onions, peeled and sliced
2 tablespoons butter
$\frac{1}{4}$ teaspoon chilli powder
1 tablespoon flour
$\frac{2}{3}$ cup chicken stock
14 oz can tomatoes
$15\frac{1}{4}$ oz can kidney beans, drained

Cooking Time: 55 minutes
Oven: 350°F

Heat the oil in a frying pan, season the chicken and fry until golden brown. Transfer to a casserole. Fry the onions in the butter, then stir in the chilli powder and flour. Slowly add the stock and bring to the boil. Add the tomatoes and the beans, season well and bring to the boil. Pour over the chicken in the casserole, cover and put in the oven to cook for 45 minutes.

Chicken and peanuts

5 tablespoons oil
1 onion, peeled and diced
Salt and freshly ground black pepper
2 tablespoons flour
4 chicken joints
$\frac{2}{3}$ cup chicken stock
$\frac{2}{3}$ cup milk
1 tablespoon peanut butter
2 tablespoons light cream

To garnish:
$\frac{1}{2}$ cup salted peanuts
Watercress sprigs

Cooking Time: $1\frac{1}{4}$ hours
Oven: 350°F

Heat the oil, sweat the onion for a few minutes and transfer to a casserole. Season the flour and coat chicken well, fry until golden brown and transfer to casserole. Add the stock to the frying pan, stir well and scrape off juices, add milk and peanut butter and heat. Pour over chicken and onion. Cover and cook in the oven for 1 hour. Taste and adjust seasoning, add cream and coat each piece of chicken with sauce and garnish with peanuts and watercress sprigs.

Chicken paella

Chicken paella

4 tablespoons oil
2 onions, peeled and sliced
1 green pepper, seeded and sliced
4 tomatoes, peeled and sliced
1 clove garlic, crushed
4 chicken drumsticks
Salt and freshly ground black pepper
1 cup rice
$\frac{1}{4}$ teaspoon saffron or turmeric
1 can crabmeat
$\frac{1}{4}$ lb shrimps
$\frac{1}{2}$ cup frozen peas
Mussels (optional)
2 tablespoons white wine (optional)

To garnish:
Finely chopped parsley

Cooking Time: $1\frac{1}{4}$ hours
Oven: 350°F

Heat the oil in a frying pan and add the onions, pepper, tomatoes and garlic. Sauté gently for a few minutes. Transfer to a casserole and then brown the chicken pieces, add to casserole, season well and cook, covered, for 30 minutes. Meanwhile cook the rice with the saffron in boiling salted water, do not cook through but remove after about 10 minutes, drain. Remove chicken and keep hot. Mix rice with vegetables in casserole, add crabmeat and shrimps and peas, replace chicken, season well and cook for another 40 minutes, covered. Taste and adjust the seasoning. If using mussels wash well and remove the beards, cook over a high heat in wine to open shells. Always discard mussels which do not open. Cover and cook over low heat for 20 minutes. Serve with mussels surrounding rice and chicken. Sprinkle with chopped parsley.

Rich chicken casserole

Rich chicken casserole

1 chicken, quartered or 4 pieces
2 tablespoons oil
2 large onions, peeled and sliced
1 medium-sized carrot, peeled and sliced
$\frac{1}{4}$ lb slab bacon, rinded and diced
Salt and freshly ground black pepper
6 tablespoons red wine
$1\frac{1}{4}$–2 cups chicken stock
Bouquet garni
1 bay leaf
6 small onions, peeled
4 mushrooms, peeled and sliced
3 tablespoons butter
2 tablespoons flour
2 tablespoons cream
Chopped parsley to garnish

Cooking Time: 1 hour
Oven: 325°F

Fry the chicken in oil until golden to seal in the juices, place in the bottom of a casserole. Fry the sliced onions, carrot and bacon, then add to the casserole. Season. Add 4 tablespoons red wine, stock, bouquet garni and bay leaf. Put into the oven for 1 hour. Simmer the whole, small onions in the remaining wine, until tender. Sauté the mushrooms in 1 tablespoon butter. Remove both and keep warm. Melt the remaining butter, add the flour and cook for a few minutes. Blend in the wine from the onions, together with some stock from the casserole, to make a smooth liquid consistency. Add to the casserole, adjust seasoning. Add onions and mushrooms 15 minutes before serving. Taste and adjust the seasoning. Remove bouquet garni and bay leaf. Stir in the cream at the last minute. Garnish with chopped parsley if liked.

Farmhouse chicken

3 tablespoons butter
3 lb chicken
2 stalks celery, washed and sliced
6 small onions, peeled and sliced
2 carrots, peeled and sliced
1 small turnip, peeled and sliced
1¼ cups chicken stock
Salt and freshly ground black pepper

Cooking Time: 1½ hours
Oven: 375°F

Melt the butter in a casserole and fry the chicken lightly on all sides. Add the sliced vegetables, stock and seasoning. Cover with a lid or foil. Braise about 1½ hours until tender, basting occasionally with the stock. Taste and adjust the seasoning. Thicken gravy if necessary.

Braised chicken with peaches

2 tablespoons oil
4½ lb chicken
Salt and freshly ground black pepper
2 tablespoons butter
2 onions, peeled and sliced
2 carrots, peeled and sliced
¼ lb slab bacon, rinded and cut into pieces
¼ teaspoon thyme
1 bay leaf
1¼ cups peach juice
8 peach halves
2 teaspoons cornstarch

To garnish:
4 parsley sprigs

Cooking Time: 1½ hours
Oven: 350°F

Heat the oil and brown the chicken. Season well and insert butter into body, transfer to a casserole. Sweat the onions and carrots in the oil left from the chicken and add bacon, put into the casserole. Add thyme, bay leaf and peach juice, season well, cover and cook in the oven for 1½ hours. Taste and adjust the seasoning. Cut the chicken into joints and place on a serving plate surrounded by halved peaches, return to oven to heat. Remove fat by skimming. Thicken sauce with cornstarch, strain and pour over or serve separately. Garnish with sprigs of parsley.

Chicken with walnuts

1 chicken, quartered or 4 pieces
4 tablespoons butter
1 leek, washed and sliced
4 small white onions, peeled
2 cups chicken stock
1 sprig thyme
2 tablespoons wine vinegar
Salt and freshly ground black pepper
⅓ cup chopped walnuts

To garnish:
Finely chopped parsley
Walnut halves
1 tablespoon cream (optional)

Cooking Time: 50 minutes
Oven: 350°F

Fry the chicken parts in the butter until golden brown, drain and place in a casserole. Toss the sliced leek and whole onions in the butter. Place the vegetables, stock, thyme and wine vinegar over the chicken. Season well. Cover and cook for 30 minutes. Remove the chicken and keep hot. Purée the walnuts with the onion mixture and some of the liquid. Pour over the chicken in the casserole and cook for 15 minutes. Taste and adjust the seasoning. Garnish with parsley and walnut halves and drizzle with cream.

Casseroled turkey with red wine

7–8 lb small turkey
½ teaspoon allspice
Finely grated rind of 1 lemon
4 tablespoons butter
Salt and freshly ground black pepper
8 small onions, peeled
1 bay leaf
1 sprig or ¼ teaspoon thyme
Parsley sprig
1¼ cups red wine
½ lb mushrooms, washed
⅔ cup cranberries, puréed

Cooking Time: 2½ hours approx.
Oven: 400°F then reduce to 325°F

Remove giblet bag, if inside, from turkey and make the contents into stock with a little water. Sprinkle the inside of the bird with allspice, lemon rind and 1 tablespoon butter. Rub remaining butter all over the turkey and season well. Place the turkey on its side to brown in a hot oven, with onions. Turn over after 15 minutes. Transfer bird and onions when brown into a casserole or, if you do not have one which is large enough, use the roasting pan covered with foil. Reduce heat to 325°F. Take 2½ cups of giblet stock, add herbs and wine, heat and pour over the bird and onions. Cook in a fairly moderate oven for 1½ hours. Cook the mushrooms for the last 15 minutes with bird. Test for readiness by pricking with a skewer, juice should be clear not pink, to indicate turkey is cooked. Carve and serve on a heated serving dish. Remove the bay leaf and herbs. Thicken gravy with a beurre manié (see page 7) whisked in, then add puréed cranberries to the sauce and pour over the turkey. Serve with a green salad with walnuts.

Chicken mexico

3–4 lb chicken
3 tablespoons butter
2 tablespoons oil
2 large onions, peeled and sliced
2 cloves garlic, crushed
1 green pepper, seeded and sliced
1 chilli pepper
1 cup canned tomatoes
2 tablespoons tomato paste
1¼ cups chicken stock or stock and wine
¾ cup corn kernels
4 tablespoons sour cream
¼ lb mushrooms, washed and sliced
Finely chopped parsley

Cooking Time: 1½ hours
Oven: 325°F

Brown the chicken in butter and oil on all sides. Remove from fat and place in a casserole. Fry onions, garlic, pepper and chilli. Add tomatoes, tomato paste and the stock and wine. Pour over the chicken and cook in covered casserole in the oven for 1¼ hours. Allow chicken to cool in the juice, then carve and put on a serving dish and keep hot. Meanwhile heat the corn. Boil up the sauce until reduced by half, add cream and stir. Add mushrooms and cook for a few minutes. Pour over chicken with parsley and sweet corn. Serve with rice.
(Ideal to make the day before and be really organized for your guests. Chicken is really best left overnight in sauce in the refrigerator.)

Duck with cherries; Chicken with grapefruit; Tarragon chicken; Chicken normande

Duck with cherries

1 duck
1 onion, peeled
1¼ cups stock
Finely grated rind of 1 lemon
Salt and freshly ground black pepper
17 oz can dark cherries
1 tablespoon cornstarch

To garnish:
Watercress sprigs (optional)

Cooking Time: 1½ hours
Oven: 375°F

Place the duck in the casserole with the onion, cover and cook with the stock for 30 minutes. Remove the liquid from the casserole and retain. Sprinkle with grated lemon rind and seasoning. Pour over the cherries, retaining a few for the garnish, and juice. Cover and cook for 1 hour or until the duck is cooked. Skim fat from first cooking liquid and thicken with cornstarch. Add to the casserole and cook for another 5 minutes. The sauce may be served from the casserole or may be put through a blender, as preferred. Garnish with fresh watercress, if liked, and whole cherries if available.

Tarragon chicken

2 tablespoons butter
¼ lb slab bacon, rinded and chopped
2 onions, peeled and sliced
2 carrots, peeled and sliced
1 chicken, quartered, or 4 pieces
2 chicken livers (optional)
3 tarragon sprigs
1¼ cups chicken stock
1 tablespoon sweet sherry
Salt and freshly ground black pepper
1 teaspoon cornstarch

To garnish:
Tarragon sprigs (optional)

Cooking Time: 1 hour
Oven: 325°F

Melt the butter in a frying pan and add the bacon, onions and carrots, cook for a few minutes, transfer to a casserole. Brown the chicken on both sides and transfer to the casserole. Finally brown the chicken livers and place around chicken. Add tarragon, stock, sherry, seasoning, cover and cook in the oven for 1 hour. Thicken gravy with cornstarch and pour back over chicken. Taste and adjust the seasoning. Garnish with fresh tarragon if available.

Chicken normande

¼ cup dark raisins
4 tablespoons butter
1 chicken, quartered, or 4 pieces
Salt and freshly ground black pepper
1½ lbs apples, peeled, cored and sliced
⅔ cup heavy cream
2 tablespoons lemon juice
2 tablespoons cider
½ teaspoon cinnamon

Cooking Time: 1¼ hours
Oven: 325°F

Soak the raisins for 45 minutes in warm water. Heat half the butter in a frying pan and brown the chicken pieces on all sides. Remove to a plate and season well. Add remaining butter and toss in the apple slices so that they become lightly browned only. Place half the apples in the bottom of a casserole and arrange chicken on top. Mix the cream with the lemon juice, cider, salt and freshly ground pepper, cinnamon and raisins. Add remaining apples round the chicken, season and pour the cream over the chicken and apples. Cover and cook in the oven for about 1 hour. Taste and adjust the seasoning.

Chicken with grapefruit

2 tablespoons butter
1 chicken, quartered, or 4 pieces
Salt and freshly ground black pepper
2 teaspoons brandy
1¼ cups chicken stock
2 tablespoons sherry
1 teaspoon tarragon
1 grapefruit
1 tablespoon cornstarch
2 tablespoons sugar

To garnish:
Watercress sprigs

Cooking Time: 1¼ hours
Oven: 325°F

Melt butter in a frying pan and brown chicken on all sides. Remove to a casserole or brown in casserole, season well. Heat brandy in a ladle and set alight, remove chicken from heat and pour over the brandy. Add the stock and sherry and tarragon, cover and cook in the oven for 1 hour. Meanwhile remove thin strips of grapefruit peel with a sharp knife. Cut the grapefruit across the top and cut round skin removing all the white pith. Cut into each segment to obtain a slice without skin. Squeeze remaining grapefruit with the hand into the casserole juice. Taste and adjust the seasoning. Thicken stock if necessary with the cornstarch. Add the sugar, strips of grapefruit peel and grapefruit segments, reserving a few for garnish, if liked. Garnish chicken with watercress sprigs and grapefruit segments if available.

CHICKEN
Boned chicken with apricots

3 lb chicken, boned
16 oz can apricot halves, drained
Salt and freshly ground black pepper
4 tablespoons butter
1 tablespoon finely chopped parsley
2 onions, peeled and thinly sliced
1 clove garlic, crushed
⅔ cup white wine
Chopped parsley (optional)

Cooking Time: 1½ hours
Oven: 350°F

This is a special dinner party dish which requires a boned chicken, but it is easy to prepare in advance.
Bone the chicken by cutting down the backbone and easing flesh away. Cut round leg joints and push flesh down, removing sinews, remove thigh bone. Keep bird on its front and ease all flesh off until the carcass is released from breast bone. Save some apricot halves for garnish. Stuff pairs of apricot halves with 2 tablespoons of butter seasoned with salt and pepper and parsley. Arrange pairs down the center of the chicken. Season well and sew up leaving no holes. Melt the remaining butter and brown the chicken on all sides, turn down heat, add onions and garlic and cook for a few minutes. Season well, add white wine and apricot juice, cover and cook in the oven for 1 hour. Remove string before serving. Serve garnished with remaining apricots, parsley, and the golden brown sauce which should be poured over. This is a very easy dish to carve for a dinner party.

Turkey in riesling

2 tablespoons butter
4 turkey legs or portions
4 scallions, washed and chopped
¼ lb mushrooms, washed and sliced
Salt and freshly ground black pepper
⅔ cup riesling wine
¼ cup heavy cream

To garnish:
Finely chopped parsley

Cooking Time: 1¼ hours
Oven: 350°F

Heat the butter in a frying pan and brown the turkey on all sides, lower heat and add scallions and sliced mushrooms. Transfer to a casserole, season well. Add wine, cover and cook for 45 minutes, add cream and cook for another 15 minutes. Taste and adjust the seasoning. Serve sprinkled with chopped parsley.

Braised turkey with mushrooms

2 tablespoons butter
1 onion, peeled and sliced
1 clove garlic, peeled and crushed
2 lb rolled turkey breast
¼ teaspoon nutmeg
Salt and freshly ground black pepper
½ lb mushrooms, washed and sliced
1¼ cups chicken stock
Bouquet garni

To garnish:
Finely chopped parsley

Cooking Time: 1 hour
Oven: 350°F

Melt the butter in a casserole and sweat onion and garlic for a few minutes. Add rolled turkey breast, sprinkle with nutmeg and seasoning. Add mushrooms, pour on the stock, add bouquet garni. Cover and cook in the oven for 1 hour. Remove the bouquet garni. Carve and serve breast slices covered with mushrooms on a heated plate. Reduce stock and thicken with 1 tablespoon beurre manié, if desired (see page 7). Garnish with chopped parsley if liked.

This is a term which applies to animals and birds which are hunted at certain times of the year and protected during breeding times. Squab, rabbits, hare and venison are available most of the year and are excellent in casseroles. Pheasant, grouse and partridge are also excellent cooked in a casserole as they can be dry when roasted unless cooked very carefully. It is now possible to buy game ready prepared and frozen in supermarkets and it is well worth experimenting to add variety to the menu.

Pheasant with mushrooms and onions

1 pheasant
2 tablespoons oil
2 tablespoons butter
2 large onions, peeled and thinly sliced
3 carrots, peeled and thinly sliced
$\frac{1}{4}$ teaspoon thyme
$\frac{1}{4}$ teaspoon chervil
$\frac{1}{4}$ teaspoon rosemary
$\frac{1}{4}$ teaspoon parsley
2 bay leaves
$1\frac{1}{4}$ cups water
$1\frac{1}{4}$ cups red wine
1 tablespoon brandy
Salt and freshly ground black pepper
2 tablespoons butter
8 small white onions, peeled
8 whole mushrooms, washed

Beurre manié
2 tablespoons butter blended with
3 tablespoons flour
2 tablespoons heavy cream

To garnish:
Watercress sprigs

Cooking Time: $1\frac{1}{2}$ hours
Oven: 325°F

Cut the pheasant into 4 serving portions with poultry shears or the butcher will do this for you. Heat the oil and butter in a frying pan. Add the onions and carrots and cook over a gentle heat for 5 minutes. Add herbs, stir well and transfer to a casserole. Sauté the pheasant in the remaining fat on a fairly high heat, turning round to brown evenly. Remove the bird to casserole. Add water to the frying pan with half the wine and heat so that all sediment is removed from frying pan. Heat brandy in a ladle, set alight and pour over the pheasant. When the flames have died away, pour over the wine mixture from the frying pan and season. Place in the oven uncovered for 1 hour, basting with juice from time to time. Meanwhile melt the butter in the frying pan, add the small onions and cook for 5–7 minutes over a low heat, but do not allow to become too brown. Add mushrooms and remaining wine, stir round in the pan and cover. Allow to cook gently for 10 minutes until wine is reduced to a glaze. Remove bay leaves. Remove the pheasant to a serving dish and keep warm. Reduce the liquid by half and thicken with the beurre manié. Add the onions and mushrooms and cook gently for 2–3 minutes. Taste and adjust the seasoning. Finally stir in cream and pour over pheasant. Garnish with watercress sprigs.

Pheasant casserole in red wine

Pheasant casserole in red wine

1 pheasant
1 tablespoon butter
1 tablespoon oil
2 onions, finely chopped
1 clove garlic, peeled and crushed
1 carrot, peeled and diced
2 stalks celery, washed and sliced
Pinch marjoram and thyme
1 bay leaf
Salt and freshly ground black pepper
$\frac{2}{3}$ cup red wine
$\frac{2}{3}$ cup stock or water

Beurre manié
1 tablespoon butter blended with 1 tablespoon flour

To garnish:
Watercress sprigs (optional)

Cooking Time: 1¼ hours
Oven: 350°F

Brown whole pheasant in butter and oil, transfer to casserole. Place vegetables in frying pan and sauté gently for 5 minutes. Turn into the casserole. Add herbs, seasoning, wine and stock to frying pan, scrape down pan juices and pour into casserole. Cook for 1 hour until tender.

Remove pheasant to a clean casserole or dish and keep warm. Skim fat from the sauce, remove bay leaf and reduce by half, then thicken by whisking in beurre manié. Taste and adjust the seasoning. Pour over the pheasant and garnish with watercress sprigs, if liked.

Squab casserole

Squab casserole

¼ lb slab bacon, rinded and diced
2 tablespoons butter
4 small squab, plucked and cleaned,
feet removed
2 small onions, peeled and sliced
1 carrot, peeled and sliced
¼ lb mushrooms, washed and sliced
⅓ cup flour
2½ cups stock
Salt and freshly ground black pepper

Forcemeat balls: (optional)
1¼ cups fresh breadcrumbs
4 tablespoons rendered suet
1 tablespoon finely chopped parsley
Grated rind ½ lemon
Salt and freshly ground black pepper
1 egg, beaten, to bind

To garnish:
Triangles of toast
Chopped parsley

Cooking Time: 1¼ hours
Oven: 350°F

Fry the bacon in heated butter until brown, remove to a casserole. In the same pan, fry the squab until brown, place in the casserole. Fry the onions, carrot and mushrooms lightly, drain and remove to the casserole. Stir in flour to frying pan, heat gently until brown, stirring all the time. Add the stock, season to taste and bring to the boil and pour into casserole. Cover and cook in the oven until tender. Mix up ingredients for forcemeat and form into small balls, add to the casserole and cook for a further 15 minutes.
Serve garnished with triangles of toast and chopped parsley.

Rabbit casserole

1 rabbit, cut into pieces
1 tablespoon seasoned flour
$\frac{1}{8}$ lb slab bacon, rinded and chopped
2 tablespoons butter
1 tablespoon oil
12 small onions, peeled
2 stalks celery, washed and sliced
1 red pepper, seeded and cut into strips
$\frac{1}{4}$ cup white wine
$\frac{2}{3}$ cup chicken stock
2 rosemary sprigs or $\frac{1}{2}$ teaspoon dried rosemary
Salt and freshly ground black pepper

Beurre manié
1 tablespoon butter blended with
1 tablespoon flour

To garnish:
Finely chopped parsley (optional)
1 tablespoon light cream (optional)

Cooking Time: 1 hour
Oven: 300°F

Prepare the rabbit and dip in seasoned flour. Place the bacon in the butter and oil and sauté gently. Remove to a casserole. Place the rabbit in the fat and brown on all sides. Transfer to the casserole. Sauté the onions gently, then add to the bacon. Sauté the celery and pepper gently and add to the casserole. Pour over the wine, stock, rosemary and seasoning. Cover and cook in the oven for at least 1 hour. Serve the rabbit on a heated serving dish with the whole onions. Thicken the sauce with the beurre manié and whisk well until smooth. Pour over the rabbit and serve with parsley and swirls of cream, if liked.

Rabbit casserole

Jugged hare

1 hare with blood
4 thick slices bacon
2 tablespoons butter
2 onions, peeled and finely diced
2 carrots, peeled and finely diced
2 stalks celery, washed and thinly sliced
1 bay leaf
1 sprig parsley or $\frac{1}{4}$ teaspoon dried
1 thyme sprig or $\frac{1}{4}$ teaspoon dried
Salt and freshly ground black pepper
$4\frac{1}{3}$ cups stock
2 tablespoons redcurrant jelly
$\frac{1}{4}$ cup port

To garnish:
1 tablespoon finely chopped
parsley (optional)

Cooking Time: $3\frac{1}{2}$ hours
Oven: 325°F

Joint the hare or ask the butcher to do it for you. Retain the blood. Gently fry bacon slices in a frying pan until the fat runs out. Remove bacon to a casserole and fry pieces of hare until golden brown, remove to the casserole. Add butter to the frying pan and cook the vegetables gently for about 3–4 minutes. Add the vegetables to the hare in the casserole with the herbs and season well. Boil up the stock in the frying pan and pour into the casserole, cover and cook in the oven for $2\frac{1}{2}$–3 hours, until hare is tender. Strain the gravy from the casserole, remove hare on to a heated dish. Return juice to the casserole, add the redcurrant jelly and port, bring to just under boiling point, simmer for a few minutes, taste and adjust the seasoning. Remove from the heat, gradually stir in the blood and reheat without allowing to boil. Strain the sauce over the hare and sprinkle with chopped parsley, if liked.

Jugged hare

It is usual to cook vegetables quickly to avoid loss of nutrients but many vegetables are excellent in casserole dishes and can even be cooked as a main meal to add variety to our menu planning. Firm vegetables such as peppers, celery, squash and zucchini are often blanched by placing in boiling water for a few minutes before being used in the casserole dish. Suffed peppers, eggplant and squash are all excellent additions to the casserole range, whether stuffed with rice, chicken or meat.

Country vegetable casserole; Potato and tomato casserole; Cabbage and celery casserole

Potato and tomato casserole

2 tablespoons butter
2 large onions, peeled and thinly sliced
1 clove garlic, crushed (optional)
1 lb potatoes, peeled and thinly sliced
Salt and freshly ground black pepper
1¼ cups stock

Topping:
2 tomatoes, thinly sliced
½ cup grated cheese
1 teaspoon chopped chives

Cooking Time: 1¼ hours
Oven: 325°F

Melt the butter in a frying pan and gently sauté the sliced onions and crushed garlic. Place a layer of onion and garlic alternately in a casserole with thinly sliced potatoes, seasoning well between each layer. Pour over the hot stock and cover the casserole. Put into the oven and cook until the vegetables are tender and the stock is absorbed. Top with sliced tomatoes and grated cheese. Brown under the broiler before serving and sprinkle with chopped chives. Cut into portions to serve with chops, steak or hamburgers although it is delicious on its own.

Country vegetable casserole

4 tablespoons butter
2 large onions, thinly sliced
4 new carrots, thinly sliced
1 new turnip, thinly sliced
1 leek, sliced
2 potatoes, thinly sliced
10 oz package frozen corn and
sweet peppers
Salt and freshly ground black pepper
1¼ cups stock
½ cup grated cheese

Cooking Time: 1 hour
Oven: 350°F

Melt the butter in an ovenproof casserole. Toss in the sliced onions and leave on a low heat for about 5 minutes. Add the thinly sliced vegetables and corn and sweet peppers with seasoning between each layer. Pour over the stock, cover the casserole and cook in the oven for 45 minutes or until the vegetables have absorbed the stock. Sprinkle with the grated cheese and brown under the broiler.

Cabbage and celery casserole

4 tablespoons butter
1 small onion, peeled and sliced
1 small head celery, washed and sliced
½ small white cabbage, washed
and shredded
2 tablespoons butter
3 tablespoons flour
1¼ cups milk
Salt and freshly ground black pepper
½ cup fresh white breadcrumbs
2 tablespoons butter

Cooking Time: 30 minutes
Oven: 350°F

Melt the butter in a frying pan, add the onion and celery and cook gently for 5 minutes, stirring from time to time. Add the cabbage and allow to simmer on a gentle heat for another 5 minutes. Melt the butter in a saucepan and add the flour to make a roux. Add the milk gradually, stirring with a wooden spoon until a smooth sauce is formed. Season well. Turn the vegetables into a casserole and season well. Pour the sauce over the vegetables and sprinkle with breadcrumbs dotted with butter. Cook in the oven for 20 minutes until the crumb topping is golden brown.

Stuffed cabbage leaves

8 large cabbage leaves
½ cup rice, cooked
¼ lb cooked chicken meat
1 tablespoon mixed vegetables
1 small onion, finely diced
Few drops Tabasco sauce
Salt and freshly ground black pepper

Tomato sauce:
1 onion, finely diced
1 tablespoon oil
16 oz can tomatoes
⅔ cup chicken stock
2 teaspoons oregano
Few drops Tabasco sauce
1 tablespoon tomato paste
1 teaspoon lemon juice
Salt and freshly ground black pepper

Cooking Time: 35 minutes
Oven: 350°F

Blanch cabbage leaves. Mix all other ingredients well and spoon out into portions on to cabbage leaves. Tie the leaves up into "parcels" with fine string or fasten with toothpicks. Place in casserole dish.
To make the tomato sauce, sauté the onion in the oil for 4–5 minutes. Add all other ingredients and bring to the boil. Taste and adjust the seasoning. Now pour the sauce mixture through a strainer over the stuffed cabbage leaves and cook in the oven for 25 minutes.

Artichokes au gratin

1 lb Jerusalem artichokes
1¼ cups milk
1¼ cups water
½ teaspoon salt
¼ lb mushrooms, washed and chopped
1 onion, peeled and diced
2 tablespoons butter
3 tablespoons flour
Salt and freshly ground black pepper
2 tablespoons light cream
¼ cup fresh breadcrumbs
¼ cup grated cheese

Cooking Time: 40 minutes
Oven: 350°F

Peel the artichokes and place in a saucepan with the milk, water and salt. Bring to the boil slowly and simmer for 10 minutes or until tender. Arrange in a casserole, cover with the mushrooms and onion. Melt the butter in a saucepan, add flour to make a roux, then pour in 2 cups of the artichoke liquid, stir well until you have a thin sauce, season well. Pour into the casserole and cook in the oven, covered, for 15 minutes. Remove the lid, sprinkle with the cream, breadcrumbs and grated cheese, return to the oven for another 15 minutes.

Mushrooms à la grecque

½ lb mushrooms, washed and sliced
1 onion, peeled and sliced
2 tablespoons olive oil
1 tablespoon tomato paste
2 bay leaves
6 peppercorns
⅔ cup chicken stock
2 tablespoons dry white wine
Salt and freshly ground black pepper

Cooking Time: 30–40 minutes
Oven: 325°F

Slice the mushrooms through the stems and blanch for 2 minutes. Sauté the onion in the oil. Arrange the mushrooms in a casserole and add the remaining ingredients. Cover and cook in the oven for 30–40 minutes. Remove bay leaves, if liked, and peppercorns. Serve sprinkled with paprika and chopped parsley.

Fish has fairly tender flesh and it is therefore unnecessary to give it long, slow cooking in most cases but whole fish and thick steaks can be casseroled for ease of cooking.
Fish stock can be made from heads, tails, bones, placed in water.
2 lb fish pieces – 2¼ quarts water, 2 onions, peeled and sliced, 1 carrot, peeled and sliced, 1 stalk of celery, washed and sliced, ⅔ cup dry white wine, ¼ teaspoon salt, 12 peppercorns and a bouquet garni.
Most fish can be poached in a fish stock and the poaching liquid can then be used to make a sauce to accompany the fish.

Fish with grapes

6 oz green grapes, halved and seeded
1 lb flaked white fish, cooked in milk
2 tablespoons heavy cream
Salt and freshly ground black pepper
1 lb potatoes, cooked and mashed
1 egg, beaten
2 tablespoons milk
1 cup grated cheese
2 tablespoons butter

To garnish:
Green grapes, halved and seeded

Cooking Time: 20 minutes
Oven: 350°F

Butter a casserole. Arrange seeded grapes over the bottom of dish. Mix fish with milk, cream and seasoning and place over grapes. Mix potato with the egg and milk, season and place over the fish. Score the top with a fork. Cover and bake for 20 minutes. Remove cover. Sprinkle with cheese and dot with the butter and broil until brown. Garnish with green grapes.

Salmon with hollandaise sauce

4 lb salmon trout, or 4 thick
salmon steaks
Salt and freshly ground black pepper
Fish stock (see above)
2 tablespoons white wine

Hollandaise sauce:
3 tablespoons wine vinegar
6 peppercorns, slightly crushed
Bay leaf
Blade of mace
2 egg yolks
¼ lb butter

To garnish:
Asparagus spears (optional)
Hard-boiled egg (optional)

Cooking Time: 30 minutes
Oven: 325°F

Clean the salmon trout and wash under the cold tap. If the scales have not been removed, leave them intact as they give protection. Place in a casserole, season and pour the stock over the fish with a little extra white wine if desired. (A large salmon which is too big for a casserole may be cooked between two large roasting tins if you do not have a fish poacher.) If using steaks place in the casserole and cover with the stock in the same way. Cover and cook in the oven. Serve hot garnished with asparagus or hard-boiled egg and Hollandaise sauce.
To make the sauce: Put the vinegar, slightly crushed peppercorns, bay leaf and mace in a saucepan and reduce over a medium heat until only 1 tablespoon remains. Place the egg yolks in a bowl with a knob of butter and beat together. Add the liquid and place bowl over a saucepan of hot water. Stir all the time and gradually add remaining softened butter, a little at a time until it is all added. A rich buttery sauce results, adjust seasoning. A few drops of lemon juice can be added if sauce is too thick. Do not leave the sauce over hot water or it will begin to set after it is cooked.

Sole with prawns; Smoked haddock and bacon casserole; Haddock flamenco

Haddock flamenco

1¼ lb haddock fillet, skinned
Salt and freshly ground black pepper
½ lb zucchini, washed and sliced
1 medium-sized onion, peeled and sliced
2 tablespoons butter
2 medium-sized tomatoes, skinned
and chopped
¼ teaspoon Tabasco sauce

To garnish:
4 parsley sprigs (optional)

Cooking Time: 30 minutes
Oven: 400°F

Cut haddock into 4 equal portions, and season each piece with salt and pepper. Fry zucchini and onion in butter until just tender, then stir in tomatoes and Tabasco sauce. Place portions of haddock in a casserole, then top fish with vegetables. Cover and cook in the oven until haddock and vegetables are tender. Serve garnished with sprigs of parsley, if liked.

Smoked haddock and bacon casserole

4 smoked haddock steaks
2 tablespoons butter
Freshly ground black pepper
4 thick slices bacon
⅔ cup milk

To garnish:
Slices of bread, toasted
Chopped parsley

Cooking Time: 25 minutes
Oven: 325°F

Remove the tail from the haddock and arrange in a casserole rubbed over with a quarter of the butter. Season fish well with pepper and divide remaining butter between fish and dot on top. Lay a slice of bacon on each fish. Pour in the milk and cook in the oven, covered. Make the toast and cut into triangles. Serve with the fish, garnished with chopped parsley. With a poached egg this dish makes an excellent brunch.

Sole with prawns

4 sole or flounder fillets
¼ lb peeled shrimp
Salt and freshly ground black pepper
⅔ cup fish stock
6 peppercorns
Blade of mace
2 teaspoons lemon juice
2 tablespoons butter
3 tablespoons flour
2 tablespoons light cream (optional)

To garnish:
Parsley sprigs
Lemon slices (optional)

Cooking Time: 25 minutes
Oven: 325°F

Wash and dry the fish. Divide half the shrimps between the fish fillets, season to taste, roll up, secure with toothpicks and place in a buttered ovenproof casserole. Cover with the fish stock, made by simmering the fish bones and stock in a little water. Add the spices and lemon juice and poach in the oven for 20 minutes. Remove from oven, strain liquor from fish fillets, discard spices and keep fish fillets warm.
Melt the butter in a saucepan, add the flour and cook gently for 2–3 minutes. Remove from heat, add the strained fish stock and blend until smooth. Return to the heat and cook until thick and creamy. Stir in cream and add remaining shrimps. Cook for 3 minutes, adjust seasoning and pour over hot fish fillets. Garnish with parsley sprigs and lemon slices, if liked.

Index